Nigel Cawthorne is the author of over 150 b
MH370 – The Mystery to *Sex Lives of the Kin*
was called to testify to the US Senate over *The Bamboo Cage*. *The Iron Cage* prompted questions in both houses of the British parliament. *Sex Lives of the US Presidents* got him on the *Joan Rivers Show* and *Sex Lives of the Popes* got him on the biggest chat show in Brazil. He lives in London.

Other books by Nigel Cawthorne
A Brief Guide to James Bond
A Brief History of Robin Hood
A Brief History of Sherlock Holmes
A Brief Guide to Jeeves and Wooster
A Brief Guide to JRR Tolkien
A Brief Guide to Agatha Christie – Queen of Crime
The King of Crime Writers – The Biography of John Creasey
The Empress of South America – The Irish Courtesan Who Destroyed Paraguay and Became Its National Heroine
Flight MH370 – The Mystery
The Bamboo Cage – The True Story of American POWs in Vietnam
The Iron Cage – Are British POWs Still Alive in Siberia?
Daughter of Heaven – The True Story of the Only Woman to Become Emperor of China
Takin' Back My Name – The Confessions of Ike Turner
Reaping the Whirlwind – Voices of the Enemy from World War II
Che Guevara – The Last Conquistador
Sex Lives of the Popes
Sex Lives of the US Presidents
Sex Lives of the Great Dictators
Sex Lives of the Kings and Queens of England
Sex Lives of the Hollywood Goddesses
Sex Lives of the Hollywood Idols
Sex Lives of the Great Artists
Sex Lives of the Great Composers
Sex Lives of the Hollywood Goddesses 2
Sex Lives of the Famous Gays
Sex Lives of the Famous Lesbians
Sex Lives of the Roman Emperors
Strange Laws of Old England
Curious Cures of Old England
Amorous Antics of Old England
Sex Secrets of Old England
Beastly Battles of Old England
Flight MH370: The Mystery
Vietnam: A War Lost and Won
House of Horrors: The True Story of Josef Fritzl, The Father from Hell
Jack the Ripper's Secret Confession
Jeremy Clarkson: Motormouth

Ian Fleming

Licence to Kill

Nigel Cawthorne

First published by Endeavour Press Ltd in 2014.

© Nigel Cawthorne 2014

Nigel Cawthorne has asserted his rights under the Copyright, Design and Patents Act, 1988, to be identified as the author of this work.

www.nigel-cawthorne.com

All rights reserved. This book is sold subject to the condition that it shall not be reproduced in whole or in part, in any form or by any means, electronic or mechanical, including photocopying, recording, or by any information storage and retrieval system now known or hereafter invented without written permission and without a similar condition, including this condition, being imposed on the subsequent purchaser.

ISBN 978-1502410597 (paperback)

Contents

Introduction	1
Chapter One – Fleming, Ian Fleming	3
Chapter Two – Among Spies	13
Chapter Three – The Worst Stockbroker in London	23
Chapter Four – Commander Fleming	34
Chapter Five – Gadgets and Guns	45
Chapter Six – Red Indians	57
Chapter Seven – Goldeneye	66
Chapter Eight – The Birth of Bond	73
Chapter Nine – Becoming a Bestseller	77
Chapter Ten – Bond at the Box Office	91
Epilogue – You Only Live Twice	100

Introduction

Ian Fleming had a gold-plated typewriter. He bought it to celebrate the completion of his first James Bond novel, *Casino Royale*. He also had a gold cigarette case, oxidized to look like gun-metal like the one he gave Bond in *Diamonds Are Forever* and *Octopussy*. Indeed, Ian Fleming would have been James Bond, but when he was Naval Intelligence during World War II his plans to be a man of action were constantly thwarted by his superiors who thought he was too valuable to risk losing. Nevertheless, he smoked, drank and womanized, and shared many other characteristics with his famous protagonist. Indeed, in his fourteen Bond books – with the single exception of *The Spy Who Loved Me* – the narration simply follows the derring-do of 007.

While Fleming was very conscious that his Bond books were pure fantasy, he insisted that everything in them had its foundation in reality. All the gadgets – in the books at least – he had come across in the war. The contacts he had made in the British intelligence services and the CIA also proved vital, and some of the plotlines mimic wartime operations he himself had planned.

Fleming was also a literary phenomenon. From a short thriller that was, at first, rejected, by force of will, business acumen and his huge range of contacts, he built Bond into a worldwide franchise that seems set to continue long into the future. His fans included John F.

Kennedy, John Betjeman, Raymond Chandler, Kingsley Amis, Somerset Maugham, Noël Coward and the millions of people around the world who have read his books. James Bond is a remarkable creation, infested with many of the demons that plagued the remarkable man who created him.

Nigel Cawthorne

Bloomsbury, August 2014

www.nigel-cawthorne.com

Chapter One – Fleming, Ian Fleming

There have been numerous James Bonds – seven actors have played him in the official Eon movies alone. Everyone can conjure the image of their favourite. But there was only one Ian Fleming, always pictured wearing a bow tie and usually with a cigarette holder or a gun in his hand. Suave, sophisticated, greying at the temples, he would have made a good M. And while he spent most of his life behind a desk, he fancied himself a man of action. That ambition thwarted, he put his lust for adventure into his famous protagonist, who shared many key facets with his creator. Of his James Bond books, Ian Fleming said: "Everything I write has a precedent in truth."

It is easy to imagine that both James Bond and Ian Fleming were quintessential Englishmen. Both are Scots. Fleming's grandfather, Robert Fleming, left school at thirteen to become a bookkeeper for a Dundee jute merchant. Spotting the young man's financial acumen, Fleming's employer sent him to represent the firm in the United States.

After the Civil War, America was short of capital. On his return to Dundee, Robert Fleming set up a pioneering investment trust to buy US railroad bonds. It was immediately oversubscribed. The trust was so successful that, within fifteen years, he was moved to London where Robert Fleming and Company, a private bank, continued to flourish for over a century. But he did not forget where he came from. He helped out poor relations and gave £155,000 to the city of Dundee to clear up the slums.

With his growing family, Robert Fleming moved into a large house in London's Grosvenor Square, later demolished to make way for the US embassy. In 1903, he bought a run-down estate at Nettlebed in Oxfordshire along with the nearby seventeenth-century mansion Joyce Grove which he had knocked down to make way for a massive red-brick palazzo with forty-four bedrooms and a dozen bathrooms. It was emblazoned with the family motto "Let the deed shaw" and generally judged a monstrosity. Nevertheless it was home to family gatherings until Ian's grandfather died in 1933. Queen Mary was also a frequent visitor who "admired" certain *objets d'art*, expecting then to be given them.

Robert Fleming and his Dundonian wife Katie had four children – Ian's father Valentine, born in 1883; his aunts Dorothy and Kathleen were born in 1885 and 1887; and his uncle Philip was born in 1889. Valentine and Philip were sent to Eton and Magdalen, Oxford. Val, particularly, was an outstanding student – as Ian would be reminded constantly. He was a member of the elite Eton Society, Pop, and rowed in the eight. At Oxford, he missed a rowing blue due to an unfortunate boil. He was president of the Undergraduate's Common Room and field master of the New College and Magdalen beagles for two years, later listing as his recreations in *Who's Who* "deerstalking, salmon fishing, fox-hunting…", riding to hounds in the South Oxfordshire and South Berkshire hunts.

Leaving Oxford with a second in history, Valentine read for the Bar but never practised. Instead he worked for his father's bank in the City, then went on to become the Conservative MP for South Oxfordshire in 1910, winning the seat from the Liberal Philip Morrell, husband of society hostess Lady Ottoline Morrell.

Less than a year after leaving Oxford, Valentine Fleming married Evelyn St Croix Rose at St Paul's church, Knightsbridge. She was a society beauty, later painted several times by Augustus John. From a well-connected family, she was also a water-colourist and played the violin. Otherwise she was considered frivolous, vain and snobbish, with an outlandish style of dress that later caused Ian and his brothers acute embarrassment.

Despite his reservations about Val's choice of wife, Robert settled a quarter of a million pounds on them – £15 million in today's money. They bought Braziers Park, an estate just four miles from Nettlebed. Soon after they took a lease on a property in Green Street, off Park Lane, Mayfair. Ian's older brother Peter was born there in 1907. He went on excel at school, becoming a noted writer and soldier. Ian was born the following year and lived under his brother's shadow for much of his life. Two more sons, Richard and Michael, followed in 1911 and 1913.

By then, the family's London residence had moved to Pitt House, which Val bought from Harold Harmsworth, the first Lord Rothermere. It had been the home of former prime minister William Pitt the Elder and signalled Fleming's political ambitions. In an early speech, he called for National Service on the grounds that "improvement in the national physique and in the habits of order and discipline of the country... do real good to the working classes". Commissioned in the local yeomanry, the Queen's Own Oxfordshire Hussars, Val would often play host to fellow officer and MP Winston Churchill.

Ian Lancaster Fleming took his middle name from John of Gaunt, duke of Lancaster, who his mother claimed ancestry from. She would later claim that her own family, the "wild Roses", were true Highlanders, unlike the Lowland Flemings, and would dress her sons in Rose tartan kilts.

The boys gave their parents nicknames. Their father was Mokie – one child's contraction of "Smokie", as Val smoked a pipe. Mother was Miewy, Mie or sometimes even M.

Holidaying in the West Country in August 1914, Ian met Ivar Bryce, who became a lifelong friend. Inspired by Robert Louis Stevenson, Jules Verne and Rider Haggard, they would search the local beaches and caves for treasure. Ian's father was not with them on that holiday. He had already set off to France with the British Expeditionary Force. Winston Churchill did not go with the regiment and remained behind as First Lord of the Admiralty, though his younger brother Jack accompanied Val.

In the autumn term in 1916, Ian escaped the clutches of his French governess and joined Peter at Durnford prep school, near Swanage in Dorset. The headmaster Tom Pellatt believed in allowing the boys to express themselves.

"Our police was not to suppress anything in a child," he wrote, "If there was a kink in the boy's nature, let it appear, and then you could see what it was and possibly cope with it."

Nevertheless, discipline was harsh and bullying was commonplace. There were no proper lavatories, only earth closets, and the food was appalling, made worse by wartime rationing introduced in 1917. Ian hated it.

There were compensations. There was swimming in the freshwater bathing pool and wrestling classes undertaken by the headmaster, both carried out naked. A Durnford, Fleming first played golf – a lifelong passion – with a club and balls provided by the headmaster's wife, Nell. He read to them on Sunday evenings – *The Prisoner of Zenda*, *Moonfleet* and the various adventures of Bulldog Drumond. Fleming's favourite was Sax Rohmer, author of the Fu Manchu series. He also took a fancy to the Pellatts' strapping daughter Hester.

While Ian was at prep school, his father wrote; his mother didn't. Val also wrote to Churchill after the Battle of Ypres, taking him to task for failing to stop the war.

"It's going to be a long war in spite of the fact that every single man in it wants it stopped at once," he said. "I do wonder what on earth you are doing."

While Jack Churchill managed to get himself transferred onto the staff of the commander-in-chief, Sir John French, Val stayed on at the Front. Just eight days before Ian's ninth birthday, he was hit by a shell and killed instantly. Winston Churchill wrote his obituary in

The Times, calling Valentine Fleming "lovable and charming". Politically: "He was most earnest and sincere in his desire to make things better for the great body of the people." Ian kept a copy of the obituary, signed by Churchill, on display in his various homes.

Valentine Fleming was awarded the DSO posthumously. Within the family, he became a secular saint. The boys were constantly admonished to remember him, to the extent that they were to end their nightly prayers with the words: "Please, dear God, help me to grow up to be more like Mokie."

Before he died, Ian's father had sold Braziers Park and acquired Arnisdale, an estate in Argyllshire, where Ian developed a romantic interest in Scotland and Scottish history. His widowed mother had all the rooms in the lodge there painted black. She took to widow's weeds with typical theatricality. Eve was just thirty-two. She kept Pitt House, but the bulk of her husband's estate – valued at over £265,000 – was held in trust for his children and their families. The trust also provided a handsome income for his widow, but if she married again it would be reduced to £3,000 a year. That's £130,000 a year today, but it still provided an incentive for her to stay single and she resented it. Meanwhile she took on the role of stern father as well as kindly mother. However, the boys spent more time with their grandparents. A wing of Joyce Grove became their weekend home. While Peter following in his father's footstep, hunting and fishing, Ian showed no interest. Instead, his grandmother would take him in the Rolls Royce to the local golf course at Huntercombe. He also learnt to shoot.

After prep school, Ian followed his older brother to Eton, where he excelled in athletics and rebelled, suffering beatings as a result. Traditionally, the beatings took place at noon, but once, when this coincided with the start time of an important race, Fleming had it brought forward a quarter of an hour and ran the race with shorts stained with blood.

Making no secret that he preferred his own company, he had few friends beyond Ivar Bryce. He spent his time reading, favouring Edgar Allen Poe, John Buchan and Edgar Wallace over Dickens, Thackeray and Trollope. He seized on the 1926 novel *Turbott Wolfe* by South African writer William Plomer, whose themes of interracial love and marriage cause a scandal in his homeland. They met three years later. Fleming invited Plomer to a party given by his mother and the two men became firm friends.

Fleming had little time for *The Eton College Chronicle*, which he dismissed as "very dry and proper and offering only minimal opportunity for an aspiring writer". Instead, he published a short story in his own, one-off magazine *The Wyvern*, which also included contribution from his mother's lover Augustus John and her friends, the architect Edwin Lutyens and aristocratic author Vita Sackville-West. Ian's story "The Ordeal of Caryl St George" was about a man who fakes his own suicide to shame his wife's boyfriend who is making love to her upstairs. Fleming called it "a shameless crib of Michael Arlen", author of *The Green Hat*. Another piece of Fleming's juvenilia, "The True Tale of Captain Kidd's Treasure", was said to have been destroyed.

The magazine showed some sympathy towards Fascism, recently established in Italy, and, during the General Strike, Fleming helped man the signal box at Leighton Buzzard, receiving a medal from the president of the London Midland and Scottish Railway Company. Thanks to his brother Peter's repeated attempts, Ian was eventually elected to Pop.

In his last year at Eton, Ian broke his nose playing football. This gave his looks a panache that made him more attractive to women. Soon after, he had sex for the first time, on the floor of a box in the Royalty Kinema in Windsor, an experience retold from the woman's point of view in *The Spy Who Loved Me*.

There were other escapades with girls outside school, even though this was strictly forbidden. Ian risked being expelled, so his mother decided to send him to Royal Military College at Sandhurst. But first, he was shipped out to a finishing school for young gentlemen in Kitzbühel in the Austrian Tyrol to brush up his German. He spent time skiing, rock climbing and charming the local lasses. By then, his mother had sold Pitt House and moved into three small cottages knocked into one in Cheyne Walk, Chelsea which had once belong to the painter J.M.W. Turner, and she gave birth to a daughter by Augustus John.

Before the Sandhurst entrance examination, Fleming was sent to a crammer. His tutor, Colonel William Trevor, wrote: "He is an exceptionally nice fellow – manly and sensible beyond his years… He ought to make an excellent soldier, provided always that the ladies don't ruin him."

Fleming passed sixth in the country. Among his intake at Sandhurst was Ayub Khan, who later became president of Pakistan. But the regimentation of the Military college did not suit Fleming. Weapons training, map reading and tactics would come in useful later, but he could not stand the interminable square bashing.

Worse, cadets needed written permission to visit private houses and were not allowed out after 10 pm. This did not suit Fleming who had fallen in love for the first time – with Peggy Barnard, the pretty daughter of a former Indian Army colonel. By then he had a battered two-seater Standard Tourer and he took her on fast drives down country lanes and to flashy restaurants and tea dances – though she was not the last woman to say he was no good at dancing. Again, he used reminiscences of these outings in *The Spy Who Loved Me*.

But Fleming was not destined to be a one-woman man. With a private income and a dress uniform, he was a popular escort for debutantes, though he disliked fashionable balls, preferring the informality of jazz clubs. Ignoring the Sandhurst rules, he would stay out all night at the Kit Kat or the Embassy, returning only just in time to shave and shower before morning parade.

Despite his other interests, Peggy was introduced to the family. She arrived at Sandhurst with his mother for at the annual sports day to watch Ian win the hurdles. But afterwards an old flame arrived to take Peggy to the Oxford Commemoration ball. In a fit of jealousy, Fleming headed off to a Soho club. After champagne, he had sex with the hostess in a back room. A few days later he discovered he had gonorrhoea. His mother booked him into a nursing home. While there, he sent his letter of resignation to Sandhurst, ending his military career. Once more, he had disgraced the memory of his father.

On a family holiday on the west coast of Ireland, Ian fell for a shy, bookish girl and wooed her with poetry. But he and his mother argued the whole time and, despairing, she sent him back to Kitzbühel. There he was in the charge of a former British diplomat and spy, Ernan Forbes Dennis, and his American wife, a successful novelist. Later, under her maiden-name Phyllis Bottome, she would publish *The Life Line*, a novel about a womanizing British Secret Service officer named Mark Chalmers. It came out in 1946, seven years before the first James Bond book was published.

Chapter Two – Among Spies

Forbes Dennis had been an intelligence officer in Marseilles during World War I. With the Armistice, he moved to the embassy in Vienna where he was passport officer, a traditional cover for an agent of the Special Intelligence Service – the SIS – known in wartime as MI6. He taught German, French and Russian. Ian would need these languages if he was to join the Foreign Office, which his mother had now decided offered a suitable career for her wayward son.

The school took some twenty pupils and, while it catered specifically for those intending to sit the Foreign Office entrance exams, Fleming was also encouraged to take an interest in history and European literature. He translated a German play by Klaus Mann, which his mother then had printed and bound. Called *Anja and Esther* this is acknowledged as Fleming's first published work.

In the evening the students entertained each other with tall tales and Forbes Dennis's wife Phyllis encouraged him to write. Under her mentorship, he wrote the unpublished short story "Death on Two Occasions". She gave him a key piece of advice: "If a writer is true to his characters, they will give him his plot." Otherwise he entertained himself sleeping with local girls who showed few inhibitions, saying at the time that he "never really cared much about the English girls... they didn't bathe enough and they didn't know the first thing about making love".

Nevertheless, he was still writing poems to the sweetheart he had left at home. A collection was printed under the title *The Black Daffodil*, but later he became so embarrassed by this juvenilia that he rounded up every copy and burned them.

During his stay in Austria, Fleming spoke for the first time of his ambition to write thrillers. Meanwhile he had clocked up some thrills of his own. With a passion for fast cars, he had once topped a hundred miles an hour on the open road in Oxford. He would pretend to be an agent pursued by gangsters. He imagined someone climbing out on the bonnet of a car and cutting the rope hold a heavy load on a truck in front – an incident he would use in *Moonraker*. But his Standard Tourer had met a sad end when the front was sliced off by a train at a level crossing. There are train wrecks in *Diamonds Are Forever* and *The Man With the Golden Gun*.

At the suggestion of Forbes Dennis, Fleming enrolled at Munich University in 1928, when Hitler was active in the city. After suffering a bout of depression, Fleming was sent for psychoanalysis with a leading disciple of Alfred Adler, but during their sessions he refused to say a word.

The following year, the annual family holiday was on Corsica. Peter arrived with his friend Rupert Hart-Davis, who went on to join Jonathan Cape where he published *Brazilian Adventure*, Peter's celebrated account of his travels in South America. Also on hand were a circle of actresses – Joyce Grenfell, Peggy Ashcroft and Celia

Johnson, who later became Peter's wife. Ian would pass the time playing bridge or swimming as often as five or six times a day. For him, it was a relief when the holiday was over.

The following year, Fleming moved on to the University of Geneva, where he studied psychology and social anthropology in French, and continued his study of Russian. Meanwhile, his friend Percy Muir, a bookseller in Bond Street, London, sent him titles that might interest him. Fleming also wrote with specific requests. One of the first was for a subscription to the French surrealist magazine *Transition*.

While he was in Switzerland, Fleming obtained the permission of psychologist Carl Jung to translate a treatise on Paracelsus into English. He later showed his translation to poet and critic Edith Sitwell, and they hatched a plan to write a book together on the sixteenth-century Swiss physician and philosopher, though nothing came of it.

In his spare time, he played golf and drove a Buick sports car around places that would later appear in *Goldfinger* and *On Her Majesty's Secret Service*. He also hung around cafés where he was feared for his caustic wit and, while he could discuss Goethe and Schiller, and recite passages from *The Magic Mountain* by Thomas Mann, his preferred reading was Georges Simenon, the prolific author who created Maigret. One girlfriend said he had a "cruel face" – an attribute he would give Bond. It attracted the girls of Geneva and many dismissed Fleming as a playboy.

During his summer holiday in 1930, he worked for the League of Nations, which left him sceptical about the usefulness of international bodies. He said, they "waste a great deal of money, turn out far too much expensively printed paper, and achieve very little indeed". Meanwhile, he developed a passion for Picasso prints and tracked down and bought Mussolini's passport. He also acquired an unofficial fiancée in the form of Monique Panchaud de Bottomes, the slim, chic, dark-haired daughter of a local landowner. The couple were inseparable.

Returning to London, Fleming passed the Foreign Office examines, but was not offered a post. His mother intervened again. She got him to write to Sir Roderick Jones, head of Reuters and the husband of a friend, asking for a job. Despite an elementary spelling mistake in the letter, after a month's trial he was taken on as a rewrite man.

"So far he has made an excellent impression," said news editor Bernard Rickatson-Hatt. "His languages are sound and his manners agreeable. He suffers perhaps from a slight F.O. [Foreign Office] bump."

Because of his facility for languages, Fleming was set to work monitoring the stories carried by foreign agencies. He was also assigned to update Reuters' file of obituaries, tackling five hundred in all.

Fleming still lived at home and, when Monique turned up for Christmas, his mother cold-shouldered her, scuppering any possibility of marriage. Male friends also got short shrift at Mrs

Fleming's establishment, while lovers had to be entertained in a workmate's flat. Otherwise life was not unpleasant. He swam in the International Sportsmen's Club and his correspondence issued from the St James's Club.

Through Sir Roderick, Fleming mixed in high social circles, appearing as a character in a number of novels, including *Public Faces* by the diplomat Harold Nicolson. In *Scenes from a Bourgeois Life*, Alaric Jacob, Fleming's closest friend at Reuters, portrayed him as a well-bred chancer with a Romanian baroness as a mistress, who otherwise had little time for women. According to Jacob, he "knew all about Gertrude Stein and Rilke, played bridge beautifully and skied like a ghost…"

Fortunately, his employers found him "accurate, painstaking and methodical" with a "good business interest, doubtless a family trait". In the summer of 1932, he was sent back to Munich, not to cover the antics of Hitler who was then vying for power in Berlin, but the Alpine motor trials where he would navigate for British rally driver Donald Healey. Then in early March 1933, Fleming returned to Switzerland, ostensibly for a skiing holiday with Monique, but actually to monitor German broadcasts concerning the vote in the Reichstag that gave Hitler untrammelled power. When he returned to London, Fleming wrote to Sir Rodney, pointing out he had been with the agency for a year and asked for a raise in salary.

Through an old friend from Eton, Fleming broke the story of the Metro-Vickers case – six British engineers working for the company in Russia had been charged with espionage and sabotaging a large

Soviet hydro-electric project. The story was datelined Riga to protect Fleming's informant.

Fleming was then sent to cover the trial, flying first to Berlin then taking the train on to Moscow via Warsaw. "Absolutely everything depends on our getting the story out first," he was told. Staying at the National Hotel with the rest of the press corps, he began filing colour pieces.

On 12 April 1933, he filed a pre-trial despatch, saying: "As the famous clock in the Kremlin Tower strikes twelve the six Metropolitan-Vickers English employees will enter a room which has been daubed with blue in the Trades Union Hal and thronged with silent multitudes in order to hear an impassive Russian voice read for four or five hours the massive indictment which may mean death or exile. Within the packed room there will be a feeling of the implacable working of the soulless machinery of Soviet justice calling to account six Englishmen to decide whether the Metropolitan-Vickers raid was a vast bungle or a Machiavellian coup."

During the trial itself, Fleming filed two thousand words a day and his forthright reporting put him at risk of arrest. To beat the opposition, he arranged to drop his copy from an upstairs window in the court building to a boy who rushed it to the censor, then to the telegraph office. He bought the messenger tennis shoes to speed his progress.

After the verdict – one acquitted, two given prison terms, three deported – Fleming tried to get an interview with Stalin. It was refused, but he was given a signed letter of refusal.

Although Fleming was not above tearing the telephone wires out to hamper rivals getting their stories back to London, one cabled back to Reuters in London: "SIR RODERICK JONES EYE SHOULD LIKE YOU TO KNOW THAT WE FELLOW JOURNALISTS OF IAN FLEMING WHOM NONE OF US HAD EVER MET BEFORE HIS APPEARANCE HERE TO COVER THE METVICKERS TRIAL NOT ONLY CONSIDER HIM A PUKHA [SIC] CHAP PERSONALLY BUT HAVE EXTREMELY HIGH OPINION OF HIS JOURNALISTIC ABILITY STOP HE HAS GIVEN US ALL A RUN FOR OUR MONEY."

After returning to London by train, Fleming was debriefed by a number of anonymous men at the Foreign Office. There was little he could tell them that they did not already know from his reports, but it got his name on file.

In Moscow, Fleming had developed a Bondian taste for vodka and caviar, but bad Beluga gave him a tapeworm which he called his "Loch Ness monster". Others dismissed this as hypochondria. Fleming was frequently absent from work due to migraines cause by a plate that had been placed in his nose after it had been broken at Eton. He also suffered from black melancholia.

In what Fleming called "the most momentous year of my life", he was fined three guineas in an Oxford court for driving an unlicensed car. He skipped the hearing because he was attending the World

Economic Conference. Then his mother forced him to break off his engagement, threatening to withdraw any further financial support. Monique's father threatened to sue for breach of promise. Meanwhile, he consoled himself with an older woman, the wife of a merchant banker, the flighty granddaughter of an earl and a number of actresses and entertainers, including a bubble girl named Storm who "leapt around the stage with very little on". They made love in the back of his mother's Daimler, leaving the car strewn with black boa feathers.

After being sent to Berlin to cover a plebiscite over re-armament and interview propaganda minister Joseph Goebbels, Fleming was offered the post of assistant general manager of Reuters in the Far East, based in Shanghai, at nearly three times his current salary. But first Sir Roderick want him to go to Berlin and interview Hitler. Fleming turned down the assignment.

Instead, he gave into pressure from his mother and quit Reuters to go into merchant banking. But his time at the news agency had taught him, he said, "to write fast and, above all, to be accurate". It was also the happiest time of his life.

His decision to quit Reuters had been precipitated by the death of his grandfather, Robert, who had left Valentine's children nothing in his will. Fleming's mother also planned to marry again, cutting her income – and thus any allowance she was giving him. His brother Peter was already an established travel writer. It was now time for Ian to stand on his own two feet – not hard thing to do, given his family connections in the City.

A colleague in finance said: "The odd thing about Ian is that he really had everything he could possibly have wanted – looks, brains, enough money and position. Yet he was never satisfied. He always behaved as if he were permanently deprived."

Of Fleming in the City, Alaric Jacob said: "This young man, so aristocratically *dégagé*, so courteous and well informed, could if he wished have enjoyed the best company in London. But he seemed to solicit not even the second best, but that of the more boorish finance capitalists." But throughout his adult life, Fleming had been fascinated by the world of the wealthy.

He showed no aptitude for banking, but he enjoyed the lifestyle with its golfing trips to Gleneagles – via a private train with carriages set aside for gambling and dancing – and visits to the casinos of Le Touquet and Deauville by private plane. There, he became fascinated by baccarat, a game recently introduced to fashionable society by the Prince of Wales. He loved the atmosphere of suppressed excitement in the green-baize gaming room of the casino in Deauville, the assorted ship-owners and financiers who owned it and the cool precision of the top dealers. But he always played for lowish stakes. He also took up with the daughter of an earl who found him "very grown-up, sophisticated and attractive". This time his mother approved, but when his new girlfriend visited Joyce Grove, she could not help notice the bad blood between Fleming and his mother, even labelling Ian "schizophrenic".

"He was tough and quite cruel," she said, "but at the same time he could be very sentimental. He was an emotional character who was good at suppressing his feelings."

Chapter Three – The Worst Stockbroker in London

After a year and a half, Fleming quit banking to become a stockbroker, first taking a short holiday driving around the Continent with the wife of a friend. Though Fleming showed no aptitude for stockbroking either, it brought him more rich and influential friends, lunching his clients at the Savoy or White's where he became a member in 1936. His boss was Lancelot "Lancy" Hugh Smith, cultivator of royalty and one-time lover of novelist Jean Rhys. Fleming maintained his position, as before, by buttering up older men. Smith had been in intelligence during World War I and his brother was deputy director of Naval Intelligence. His circle of friends also included newspaper proprietors Lord Beaverbrook and Lord Kemsley, along with Noël Coward and Somerset Maugham.

Fleming also maintained contacts outside the City. Through his mother he knew Augustus John, who later sketched Fleming and remained one of his heroes. Then there was the occultist, novelist and mountaineer Aleister Crowley who wrote propaganda for the Germans during World War I, though it has since been claimed he was a double agent. When visiting the Jermyn Street lair the "Great Beast", as he was known by his mother, Fleming always addressed Crowley as "Master". Through him and other contacts, Fleming kept up to date on what was happening in Germany.

Unable to do much in the office, Fleming was put to work on the firm's monthly investment newsletter, where he caused amusement by favouring the excitement of risky investments over copper-bottomed certainties. He was also employed to write a short history of the company, which was later consigned to the waste-paper bin. Colleagues complained that he was supercilious and did little for the firm. He had, for example, adopted the affectation of smoking custom-made Morland cigarettes, containing a blend of three Balkan tobaccos that had a higher nicotine content than cheaper brands. Bond would follow suit.

The company sent Fleming on a meet-the-client trip to the United States. Before leaving, he asked a friend at the publisher Chatto & Windus – whose magazine *Night and Day* Ian had invested in – for contacts among the Greenwich-Village set. Fleming was already a fan of one-time denizen F. Scott Fitzgerald, but it was assumed that he was looking for "personable wenches". As a result, he was given a letter of introduction to Bennett Cerf, the proprietor of Random House.

Staying at the St Regis with a colleague, Fleming excused himself from dinner with a client on the grounds that he was ill. Checking on him later, the colleague found Fleming in bed with a glass of whiskey and an attractive blonde. He also became fond of the night-spots of Harlem. In Washington, he visited Alaric Jacob, then Reuter's correspondent there. They had dinner the National Press Club in Washington, where the conversation turned to President

Roosevelt's foreign policy. Jacob got the distinct impression that Fleming was snooping for the intelligence services.

Fleming used any money he made from stockbroking to buy antiquarian books, a hobby he had started with the encouragement of Vanessa Hoffman, a girl he had met in Munich. His area of interest specifically concerned technical or intellectual progress since 1800. His collaborator in this enterprise was his old friend Peter Muir, who was also using the book trade to smuggle money out of Germany for Jews who intended on leaving the country. Fleming stored his collection in fifty-one black buckram boxes, each embossed with the Fleming family crest.

Through Muir, Fleming became a member of the Left Book Club, a pacifist and anti-Fascist group started by the publisher Victor Gollancz. They quit after less than a year because of the club's increasingly Marxist leanings. Fleming remained a committed anti-Fascist though. Largely, he socialized with people who opposed appeasement, those close to Churchill and others who were secretly charting the rise of German militarism. He was also the treasurer of a committee that arranged a tour of Britain for the psychologist Alfred Adler.

Fleming's mother bought a country home near Joyce Grove, where she converted the stable, which had once been home to Cromwell's troops, into a library for Peter, making a home for the peripatetic author. Meanwhile Ian had the run of Turner's House as a bachelor pad. Then Peter married the actress Celia Johnson. Mother did not approve, believing that he should have taken a wife from the aristocracy rather than an actress, or what she considered a jumped-up chorus girl. Ian tried to talk her round. It did no good. She quit her new house and moved back to Cheyne Walk. To get away from her, Ian moved into a flat in a converted Strict Baptist chapel in Ebury Street, Pimlico. He bought the lease from Oswald Mosley, head of the British Union of Fascists, whose wife, Diana Mitford, was a friend of the family. His mother said: "But Ian, darling, how stupid wanting to live in a dirty old church."

Fleming had the place decorated by Rosie Reiss, a young refugee who Peter Muir had helped escape from Germany. There were no windows. The skylight was tinted blue and the walls painted grey. In the middle of the living room was a huge black sofa and the fire was kept burning even in the middle of summer.

The flat was full of avant-garde novels, copies of the *Paris Review* and the surrealist photographs of Man Ray. Also on display were a framed copy of his father's obituary, Mussolini's passport and silver trophies Ian had won at Eton. These were to take pride of place amid an autobiographic diorama of his life so far. Underneath was a quote, in German, from the eighteenth-century German Romantic poet Novalis: "We are about to wake up when we dream that we dream." To complete the household, he had an Irish maid called Mary. Bond's housekeeper was Scottish and called May.

Female guests were entertained with kedgeree and champagne, and either seduced or repelled by his collection of French pornography, largely featuring flagellation. After breaking off his engagement, Fleming boasted that he was going to be "quite bloody minded about women from now on", claiming to be "without any scruples at all". Women found him, while good-looking, vain and supercilious. "A man with sex on the brain", he was free of shame or prudery, and would suggest sex with a woman who appeared interested on half-an-hour's acquaintanceship. One female friend said that he got off with women because he could not get on with them. Nevertheless, he managed to surround himself with the type of fresh-faced *ingénues* who would be the models for his Bond girls. There was a Rumanian countess, an American heiress, a marquess's daughter and a large lady who he nicknamed "the galloping bedstead". The brother of the daughter of a Midlands businessman turned up on the doorstep with a horsewhip. Fortunately, his sister had got wind of it, and she and Fleming spent the day in Brighton.

Fleming avoided any emotional entanglements and was discreet. He kept friends and lovers apart and was not mentioned in a divorce case until he was forty-two. Like Bond, when it came to women, he did not have to try too hard.

"Women have their uses for the relief of tension," he said. They also provided a momentary relief from loneliness. "The only time people are not alone is just after making love. Then the warmth and languor and gratitude turn them into happy animals. But soon the mind starts to work again and they become again lonely animals."

He considered women to be animals to be petted, made a fuss of, bought presents for – and something more sinister.

"So women respond to the whip, some to the kiss," he wrote. "Most of them like a mixture of both, but none of them answer to the mind alone, to the intellectual demand, unless they are a man dressed as a woman."

He certainly did not want to marry one.

"I couldn't bear my wife's eyes gradually going dull after the honeymoon and only lighting up again when she talked to her friends," he said. The only possible wife was a woman who was "double jointed, and who knew how to keep quiet and make a *sauce béarnaise*". As for children: "The main danger of breeding is that you may double the strengths but you may also double the weaknesses."

He wrote of Bond's attitude, going from one woman to another, in *Casino Royale*: "He found something grisly in the inevitability of the pattern of each affair. The conventional parabola – sentiment, the touch of the hand, the kiss, the passionate kiss, the feel of the body, the climax in the bed, then more bed, then less bed, then the boredom, the tears and the final bitterness – was to him shameful and hypocritical."

Elsewhere Fleming wrote: "As with drugs, he needs a stronger shot each time, and women are just women. The consumption of one woman is the consumption of all. You can't double the dose."

The male visitors to Ebury Street were a bunch of Old Etonians-about-town, including at least one Fascist sympathizer. Another was John Fox-Strangways, whose name Fleming appropriated as the Secret Service station chief in the Caribbean in *Live and Let Die* and *Dr. No*. He also got a name check in *Diamonds Are Forever* and *The Man with the Golden Gun*. This circle of friends came to play bridge, a game Fleming did not excel at. He was, however, fascinated by the idea of cheating at cards and a friend remembered him trying to reconstruct from memory the Culbertson hand Bond would later use to defeat Drax in the bridge battle in *Moonraker*.

They dined at his flat two or three times a month, after spending hours deliberating over the menu. He called them the *Cercle* – short for *Le Cercle gastronomique et des jeux hazard*. At weekends, they played golf and he built elaborate myths around such mundane activities. But within the *Cercle*, he talked little of writing. When questioned about it by a friend from Kitzbühel, he shrugged and said: "My brother Peter's the writer in the family and he's really terrible good at it."

By then Peter Fleming had secured his reputation with his third book *News from Tartary: A Journey from Peking to Kashmir*. Not only was Peter the writer of the family, his books had shown him to be a fully-fledged man of action.

Away from his fellow Old-Etonians, Ian was embarrassed about being a stockbroker. Feeling that he was playing second fiddle to his brother, Fleming began talking again about writing a thriller in the Sapper mould, but with villain who snorted Benzedrine, as Fleming did himself. His model at the time was Geoffrey Household's *The Third Hour*, giving copies to all his friends at Christmas. Household's hero is an Englishman with a highly developed sense of honour, though against the background of a revolution in Mexico he rapes a cold-blooded Nazi countess. Another favourite was *Three Weeks* by Elinor Glyn, the story of a torrid affair where the woman makes the running. He gave it to women friends and it is thought that he sought out the author who lived near friends in Buckinghamshire. However, no one thought that he would get round to writing a novel himself, believing that he needed the discipline of office life to get anything done.

During a visit to the International Surrealist Exhibition in London in 1938, Fleming suffered an appendicitis. After an appendectomy, paid for by his mother, he convalesced with Ivar Bryce and a girl he wanted to seduce on Capri in Fascist Italy. There he had a brief affair with a Hungarian countess. Another girlfriend gave him a cigarette case that looked like it was made of gun-metal – like James Bond's. In fact, it was made of oxidized gold.

Fleming still had some interests in journalism. After the demise of *Night and Day*, he tried to interest writer and critic Cyril Connolly in his plans to set up a British magazine along the lines of the *New Yorker*. Connolly was unimpressed. He said: "Whenever I saw Ian towards the end of his time in the City, he gave the impression of being a playboy business man with all the money and all the friends he could possibly want. I met him once in Brook Street. He was wearing a blue suit and an Eton Ramblers tie and his appearance was so absolutely correct that it made me think of someone out of a Wodehouse novel."

Now hobnobbing with the country-house set, Fleming rubbed shoulders with a mixture of people – those who were helping Jews who were fleeing Germany, appeasers, politicians, diplomats and spies. On his regular trips through Germany and Austria he kept his eyes and ears open for information, and maintained contacts with the Foreign Office and the mysterious Z Organization that recruited top businessmen as agents to work alongside the Secret Intelligence Service. John Buchan seems to have been his favourite reading at the time.

While Fleming stood up for democracy against what he called the "younger and more exciting creeds, such as Fascism and Communism", on his one visit to the House of Commons, he found the debate there degrading and infantile. If this was politics, he said, "I would much rather not see it". He never went back.

In the social round, Fleming ran across Ann Charteris, a friend of Somerset Maugham and Evelyn Waugh. They met beside a swimming pool in Le Touquet. She was a beauty with green eyes and dark hair and found him "a handsome moody creature".

Her marriage to Lord O'Neill had broken down and she was having an affair with Esmond Harmsworth, son of the newspaper proprietor Lord Rothermere. Her friends called Fleming "Glamour Boy", but he was ardent, making himself a frequent guest at her house in Montagu Square. Then in early 1939, she visited Ebury Street for dinner.

"He had a migraine," she recalled, "was unable to speak for an hour, gave me a book to read and told me to 'keep quiet till I am ready for you'. Considering the slightness of our acquaintance, very odd behaviour."

The tactic seems to have worked though.

He declined an offer to take a trip around the Balkans with her promoting British fashion in May 1939. Instead, he intended to return to Moscow, probably at the behest of the Foreign Office. With war looming, he wanted to get more involved in intelligence work. His brother Peter was already working part-time for Military Intelligence. With Peter's help, Ian was taken on by *The Times* as a special correspondent to cover a British trade mission to the Soviet Union where he bedded a young lady from Odessa.

He returned from Moscow on the Warsaw Express with Sefton Delmer, a journalist for the *Daily Express* who had interviewed Hitler and went on to run Britain's black propaganda in World War II. As they approached the Polish border, Delmer memorized his notes, then tore them up and threw them away.

"Why don't you swallow them?" mocked Fleming. "That's what all the best spies do."

When the Soviet border guards searched Fleming's luggage, they found Russian condoms which were made from artificial latex. He was bringing them back for chemical analysis so the British could judge how advanced Soviet rubber technology was. As the Soviet guard held the samples up to the light, Delmer said to Fleming with ill-concealed glee: "You should have swallowed them."

While *The Times* paid Fleming £2 18s for a piece on a visit to the opera in Moscow, they rejected his article on the state of the Soviet Union's armed forces. It was sent instead the Foreign Office. In it, he concluded that "Russia would be an exceedingly treacherous ally." His contacts in the Foreign Office concurred and called him in for a chat. Soon after, Fleming made another trip to the Continent, where he had a one-night stand with the actress Diana Napier in a wagon-lit, a scene revisited in *From Russia With Love*.

Chapter Four – Commander Fleming

Fleming's freelance spying seems to have done him no harm. Back in London, Admiral John Godfrey, director of the Naval Intelligence Department, was looking for a deputy. In May 1939, the governor of the Bank of England phoned and said: "We've found your man." Godfrey invited Fleming for lunch in the Carlton Grill and asked him to hold himself in readiness for a very special post when the war came, but would not tell him what the job entailed. An official letter from the Admiralty a few days later left him none the wiser.

Godfrey then phoned and, after a further meeting in the Admiralty itself, he asked Fleming if he could get leave from his firm to start working in the Admiralty part-time. This was arranged and, three or four afternoons a week, after lunch in White's in St. James's, he would make his way down the Mall and present himself for duty. Godfrey was quickly impressed.

"He had a remarkable power of assimilating details of any organization," the Admiral said, "and I arranged for him to be shown everything. Within a month he had a better all-round picture of NID and its place in the Admiralty than most of the people who had been there for years."

On 26 July 1939, Fleming was given a commission in the Royal Naval Volunteer Reserve, initially as a lieutenant, later a commander

– the rank Bond would also hold. On the outbreak of war, he would be the director of Naval Intelligence's personal assistant.

"From the beginning, my idea was that I would tell Ian everything," said Godfrey, "so that if anything happened to me there would be one man who would know what was going on – he could ensure the continuity of the department. I also used him a lot to represent me on important routine inter-departmental conferences."

On 4 September, the first day of the war, Fleming appeared for dinner at Ann's house in his naval uniform, only to be teased by his friends who called him the "Chocolate Sailor" because the stripes on his sleeve made him look like the man in the current Black Magic advertisements. For once in his life, he was doing something deadly serious, though. At Room 39 in the Admiralty and in Operational Intelligence Centre deep below Whitehall, Naval Intelligence plotted German shipping movements from the intercepted signals being decoded at Station X, Bletchley Park. Fleming's Section 17 then formulated strategy and briefed Winston Churchill, initially when he was First Lord of the Admiralty and, later, when he was prime minister.

Fleming occupied a desk outside the green baize door of Admiral Godfrey's office and liaised with the other secret services, often via meetings at his club, White's. The Sandhurst drop-out and self-styled "worst stockbroker in London" had finally found his *métier*. He worked long hours, starting at six in the morning – two-and-a-half hours before his boss – then long into the night. Part of his job was to liaise with the heavily censored press. This put him back in touch with Lord Kemsley, owner of the *Sunday Times*. He was also involved in propaganda, political warfare and subversive activities. And he would visit Bletchley Park where he got to know codebreaker Alan Turing.

"He always tended to be presented with unusual jobs that no ordinary department would take responsibility for," said Admiral Denning.

Fleming also got to know the Australian pilot Sidney Cotton who undertook photo-reconnaissance work for the department. Cotton was an amateur inventor who came up with novel solutions for technical problems, along the lines of Bond's Q. Together they encouraged the use of radar, then in its infancy.

"Ian had an odd sort of imagination, always given to flights of fancy," said Cotton. "'Sidney,' he said once, 'suppose the Huns are using southern Ireland as a base for U-boats – they'd need only one or two small bays along some deserted stretch of coastline.'"

Cotton ended up photographing the entire coast of the Irish Republic from two thousand feet.

Peter Fleming was then working for Military Intelligence's dirty tricks department MI(R). Ian was to follow suit. He introduced Sefton Delmer to Admiral Godfey with a view to setting up a radio station to broadcast black propaganda to U-boat crews to sap their morale. They dreamed up other dirty tricks – producing Reichsmark coins with propaganda on the rear, forging German banknotes to sabotage the currency, making black propaganda broadcasts, spreading morale-sapping rumours and devising a plot to entrap

German secret agents after two SIS men had been seized by the Nazis in The Netherlands. Fleming also set a up scheme to buy up German merchant ships docked in neutral ports so they could not be used by the enemy. And he oversaw a plan to scuttle barges full of cement at the narrowest point of the Danube to deny Germany petrol from the Rumanian oilfields. The plan went wrong, but the department's agent Merlin Minshall escaped, in true James Bond style, on a high-speed Air Sea Rescue launch, then over the border to Trieste. However, the botched operation delivered the Nazis a propaganda coup and the Foreign Office was furious.

Minshall's enemies called him a "bloody pirate". In later life, he said of Fleming: "He was ruthless, unsure of himself and a romantic. All the qualities that I had, he wished he had. That's why he used me as his model for Bond."

An accomplished raconteur, Minshall said his mother Theodora Wigham-Richardson was a spy in the First World War and had taught him the "tactics of the trade". He claimed that he had been kidnapped by the Gestapo in 1939 and had escaped on last Orient Express before the war broke out, disguised as a doctor. The reason he had been picked for the Danube operation was that he had travelled the length on the river before the war – escaping death at the hands of a beautiful Nazi agent, according to his own account.

At the beginning of the Danube operation, Minshall had arrived in Bucharest with false-bottomed suitcases carrying detonators and high explosives wrapped in gold and red foil in an attempt to disguise them as Macintosh's toffee de luxe. After failing to bribe river pilots with gold sovereigns, he commandeered half-a-dozen British ships and had British ratings brought out to man them. But the ships had run out the fuel because the Germans had siphoned off the gasoline under cover of night. Nevertheless, Minshall claimed, he run a launch packed with high explosives into a railway embankment at high speed.

There were others involved in the caper who could have served as a prototype for Bond. One was the rugged Michael Mason, also with the RNVR. Ex-Eton and Sandhurst, he was a first-class shot and an amateur boxer. When two Nazi agents were sent to assassinate him, he killed them both. He said that he had shipped thirteen tons of gelignite out to Bucharest on the Orient Express, disguised as the ambassador's luggage. On the train, he and a Rumanian agent had tackled two men who had been watching them in the dining car.

"I knew they'd be waiting to jump me in the corridor and there they were," said Mason. "I hit one under the heart and one in the jaw and out they went. I beat them insensible and threw them off through the lavatory window."

Then there was Commander Alexander "Sandy" Glen, an alumnus of Fettes like Bond, who, while naval attaché in Belgrade, seduced the wife of a Belgian diplomat. He said: "Certainly the Admiralty recognized the importance of the Danube very early indeed, not only in itself, but in conjunction with the Rumanian oil wells, both so vital to the German economy… Captain Max Despard, whose assistant I was, played a vital part. But it is Ian Fleming who is and must be the central figure… Michael Mason had physical and mental attributes which would have stretched Bond at his very best... Dunstan Curtis had a part – elegance and courage in a nicely understated way... But much of Bond lay in Fleming himself, in his own sharp mind, his imagination and his frustrations, too, at being tied so often to a desk job as the DNI's personal assistant."

Fleming also had dealings with Commander Wilfred "Biffy" Dunderdale, the immaculately dressed SIS station chief in Paris. Wearing Cartier cuff-links and hand-made suits, he drove a bullet-proof Rolls-Royce and ran a private spy network, financed by the wealth he had inherited from his father, a shipping magnate. Dunderdale pulled off the biggest intelligence coups of the war. When he learnt of Polish cryptographers' progress in breaking the German Enigma code, he sent plans of the *"bomba"* they used to crack the code, along with two Polish copies of the Enigma machine, to London who forwarded them to Turing.

Meanwhile, Fleming's brother Peter made his first foray into light fiction with *The Flying Visit*. In the novel Hitler makes an unplanned arrival in England after his plane is shot down while he is observing a bombing raid. When Hitler's deputy Rudolf Hess mysteriously turned up in Scotland in May 1941, Peter appeared chillingly prescient. Knowing that Hess was highly superstitious, Ian tracked down his old friend Aleister Crowley, who volunteered his services to the Director of Naval Intelligence.

Peter had also seen action in Norway and was even reported killed in action at one point before he took a post parallel to Ian's as assistant to the director of Military Intelligence. Later they spent

Whitsun weekend together in Southend after intelligence had been received that the Germans were planning a raid.

Ian planned an operation in the Frisian Islands. He wrote about it in 1960 when driving to Hamburg to report on the nightlife there for the *Sunday Times*.

"The last time I had paid serious attention to these island names – Wangerooge, Spiekeroog, Nordeney, Borkum – was when, as a young Lieutenant RNVR, I had studied them endlessly on Admiralty charts and put up a succession of plans whereby I and an equally intrepid wireless operator should be transported to the group by submarine and there dug ourselves in, to report the sailings of U-boats and the movements of the German fleet."

He used this idea in the short story "From a View to a Kill" where Russian spies dig an underground observation post to watch traffic going into and out of Allied headquarters.

Fleming's Frisian plans were well advanced. "Everything in those foolhardy minutes on Admiralty dockets was thought out, everything provided for," he said. "There would be a pedal generator for the wireless set, we would live on shell-fish, my excellent (as I claimed) knowledge of German would be enough to bluff our way out of trouble in case some inquisitive fisherman turned up."

Nothing came of it. Admiral Godfrey was hardly likely to risk the capture of his highly valued deputy and Fleming did not argue with his boss.

Godfrey said of Fleming: "He learned more quickly than some of his RNVR colleagues that the NID was not a debating society, that orders must be obeyed promptly and not treated as a basis for discussion."

Godfrey noted that Fleming was equally disciplined in his personal life: "He was reticent about his own affairs and kept his friends in watertight compartments, sometimes with perplexing results. He had periods of sadness and could withdraw within himself in a way that some found baffling and disconcerting." In the circumstances this was not important. "Ian was a war winner and the country and the Navy owe a great debt to those who recommended him. I once said that Ian should have been DNI and I his naval adviser."

Fleming feared that the Germans might have put listening devices on wrecks in the Channel to transmit the noise of passing Allied shipping back to their U-boats. No one had thought of this before and a search was made of the sunken ships off the Kent coast. He also had a plan to lure the German navy out of port.

"Why not send a cruiser to Heligoland Bight with an extremely powerful transmitter?" he suggested. "It could keep up a torrent of abuse, challenging the German Naval commanders by name to come out and do something about it. No sailor likes to be accused of cowardice, and the Germans are always particularly touchy."

This was given serious consideration, but the idea was dropped when no cruiser with a powerful enough transmitter became available.

"A lot of Ian's ideas were just plain crazy," said Admiral Denning. "One had to accept an element of wildness in all his thinking. But a lot of his far-fetched ideas had just a glimmer of possibility to them that made you think twice before you threw them in the wastepaper basket. Just before the Dieppe raid, for instance, he had the idea of sinking a great block of concrete with men inside it in the English Channel to keep watch on the harbour through periscopes. We never did it, of course, but it might have worked."

Fleming did briefly become a field agent himself. When SIS pulled out of Paris, he flew in, picking up the money to sustain his two-week secondment from the cash SIS kept in the offices of Rolls-Royce in Paris. It was here that Fleming made his first contact with the Deuxième Bureau, which features in *Casino Royale*, *Goldfinger*, *On Her Majesty's Secret Service* and the short story "From a View to a Kill".

As the Germans closed in on Paris, Fleming headed on with a wireless operator to a luxurious chateau outside Tours, temporary home to French Navy Minister François Darlan. At the time the French had the fourth largest navy in the world and Churchill knew that Darlan had no great love of Britain. Replying to a toast at a dinner that the Admiralty had given the previous December, Darlan had reminded his hosts that his great grandfather had been killed at the Battle of Trafalgar. Fleming's mission was to find out from Darlan what would happen to the French Navy in the event of an armistice.

"I cannot imagine what made me suggest this," said Fleming, "except perhaps my usual desire to escape from Room 39 and get some fresh air."

Darlan failed to admit that the Battle of France was now lost, but gave Fleming some vague assurances that were transmitted to London. The chateau was then attacked by German diving bombers. Darlan and his staff fled, with Fleming and his radio operator in hot pursuit.

Then Fleming's orders suddenly changed. He was sent to Bordeaux where dignitaries, servicemen and refugees were clamouring to board ships bound for Britain. His new assignment was to stop a large dump of aero engines and spares falling into enemy hands. While other war materials were simply torched, Fleming ordered the captain of a freighter to load several dozen large crates – without telling him what they contained – ahead of a gaggle of waiting VIPs. The crates arrived safely in England two days later. Meanwhile Fleming joined the British and French general staffs at the Chapon Fin in Bordeaux, one of the finest restaurants in France. Though the atmosphere was sombre, the restaurant brought out its finest wines and most celebrated dish – all at its own expense.

Afterwards Fleming burnt documents left in the British consulate, then took the key to the American consulate nearby. When the consul said he had no authority to accept the key, Fleming simply thrust it into his pocket and said goodnight. He then spent his time organizing the evacuation of the remaining British expatriates and managed to find a berth on the last boat leaving for King Zog of Albania, along with retinue and crown jewels, who had turned up at the last moment.

Fleming has one final suggestion to make to the departing British minister to Paris.

"Why doesn't His Majesty's Government offer Admiral Darlan the Isle of Wight for the duration of the war and make it French territory under the French flag for the entire period?"

The minister merely smiled. Darlan went on to join the Vichy government, which refused to hand the French Navy over to Britain. As a result, the following month, the British bombarded the French fleet in their base at Mers-el-Kébir, Algeria, sinking most of it and killing over a thousand French sailors. Darlan was in Algiers when the Allies landed in North Africa in 1942. He gave orders that the landings should go unopposed. Nevertheless he was killed by an anti-Vichy assassin soon after, set up by the SIS.

While SIS agents and British diplomatic staff headed home, Fleming moved on to Lisbon. From there, he was to fly to Madrid to liaise with the British naval attaché. However, the only airline flying that route was Lufthansa. Initially, the German airline refused to take an officer in a British Navy uniform. But Fleming insisted. As a commercial airline, they were obliged to take him anywhere they flew to, provided he could pay for the ticket.

Chapter Five – Gadgets and Guns

After his escapade in France and Spain, Fleming returned to Room 39 with his reputation greatly enhanced. As part of his job, he kept in touch with clandestine operations as liaison officer with the Special Operations Executive set up by Churchill to "set Europe ablaze". He was in regular contact with Robert Bruce Lockhart, whose activities in post-Revolution Russia were recorded in *Memoirs of a British Agent* and then headed the Political Warfare Executive and Fitzroy Maclean, who recorded his travels in Stalinist Russia in *Eastern Approaches*, joined the SAS in North Africa and fought alongside Tito in Yugoslavia. And he arranged transport for the Free French and the Norwegians who were sending agents via the "Shetland bus" service across the North Sea into Scandinavia.

Fleming also took a lively interest in gadgets. With gunsmith Robert Churchill, he developed a gas pistol disguised as a fountain pen. It came with two cartridges, lethal and non-lethal. Bomb-maker and dirty-tricks expert Lord Suffolk taught him how to kill a man by biting the back of his neck and Charles Fraser-Smith at the Ministry of Supply showed him shoelaces that acted as saws, shaving brushes with secret compartments and hollowed-out golf balls. These would be used to transport uncut diamonds in *Diamonds Are Forever*. Fraser-Smith was the model for Major Boothroyd, the departmental armourer in *Dr No*, a character that was developed into Q in the films. Fleming also liaised with William "Wild Bill" Donovan – the World War I Medal-of-Honor winner who was to set up the US Office of Strategic Services, which later became the CIA – when he made a fact-finding trip to Britain.

Friends were found jobs in the Operational Intelligence Centre, where enemy submarines were tracked, the "secret navy" that landed agents in occupied Europe, or Bletchley Park. Early in the war, with the help of the Polish code-breaking kit sent home by Dunderdale, Bletchley Park had cracked the codes used by the German army, air force and intelligence service – the *Abwehr*. But it had not broken the more complex codes used by the German Navy, or *Kriegsmarine*. Breaking the *Luftwaffe* codes had allowed the RAF to win the Battle of Britain, but with wolf packs of U-boats sinking shipping on the North Atlantic, Britain faced starvation unless the Enigma code directing the submarines was broken. One way to do that was to capture the codes books and a German Navy Enigma machine, the portable device used to code and decode messages.

To do this, Fleming devised Operation Ruthless to capture a German boat and steal its code books. The plan was outlined in a memorandum to Admiral Godfrey, dated 12 September 1940:

I suggest we obtain the loot by the following means:

1 Obtain from Air Ministry an airworthy German bomber.

2 Pick a tough crew of five, including a pilot, W/T operator and word-perfect German speaker. Dress them in German Air Force uniforms, add blood and bandages to suit.

3 Crash plane in the Channel after making S.O.S. to rescue service in P/L [plain language].

4 Once aboard rescue boat, shoot German crew, dump overboard, bring rescue boat back to English port.

In order to increase the chances of capturing an R. or M. [*Räumboot* – a small minesweeper; *Minensuchboot* – large minesweeper] *with its richer booty, the crash might be staged in mid-Channel. The Germans would presumably employ one of this type for the longer and more hazardous journey.*

Fleming pencilled in his own name as one of the German-speaking aircrew, but again he was not allowed to go on the mission. Naval Intelligence could not risk his capture – he knew too much. Nevertheless he assembled the team in Dover but, in the end, the operation was cancelled because there were no suitable German vessels plying the Channel and it was decided that the crew would probably have drowned before they could get out of the ditched plane. Alan Turing and his assistant Peter Twinn, who were depending on this operation to help them with their code-breaking, were said to be "like undertakers cheated of a nice corpse".

Again Fleming's ambition to be a man of action had been thwarted, but he continued his social round in London, bedding women and dining out with friends who now included Prince Bernhard of the Netherlands and Martha Huysmans, the daughter of the Belgian prime minister. There was danger enough. On three occasions during the Blitz, he was narrowly escaped death when the place he was dining was hit by a bomb. Fleming was not one to retreat to an air-raid shelter. But he was not untouched by tragedy. News came that his younger brother Michael was missing in action. It was then report that he had been wounded and taken prisoner of war. Finally, news came that he was dead.

Things were going badly for the Allies and Fleming was sent back to Lisbon and Madrid on Operation Goldeneye, the planned defence of Gibraltar should Germany seek to invade via Spain. "Wild Bill" Donovan was making a trip around British facilities in the Mediterranean at the time. Fleming met up with him again and told him of the Goldeneye plans as it was vital to convince the Americans that Britain would not capitulate.

Running parallel to Goldeneye was Operation Tracer. If Gibraltar was captured by the Germans, six volunteers would stay behind, sealed inside the Rock, observing enemy movements below through two twelve-inch slits – one facing west, one east. They would have supplies for a year and there would be no way out.

In May 1941, Fleming and Godfrey flew to the US ostensibly to see William Stephenson, codenamed Intrepid, who ran British Security Co-ordination out of New York. The real purpose was to lobby for Donovan to head a new American foreign intelligence agency, taking the role away from the FBI's J. Edgar Hoover who was notoriously anti-British. They travelled in a flying boat, via Lisbon and the Azores, stopping at Bermuda where Fleming lost money to some Portuguese businessmen at the tables. Leaving the casino, Fleming turned to Godfrey and said: "What if those men had been German secret service agents, and suppose we had cleaned them out of their money. Now that would have been exciting."

This possibly inspired a scene in *Casino Royale*, though there may have been some other origins for the tale. Another member of Naval Intelligence named Ralph Izzard told Fleming about an occasion when he played roulette with expatriate Nazis in Lisbon while en route to South America on a wartime mission. Then there was Dušan Popov, the Yugoslav playboy and MI5 double agent in the *Abwehr*, who passed codes messages through the numbers he bet on in the casino in Estoril. Popov was gambling in Lisbon when a Lithuanian kept calling "*Banque ouverte*", indicating there was no upper limit on stakes. Popov put down $30,000, which belonged to MI5. The Lithuanian blanched and refused the bet. The incident became part of the Popov legend in security circles. Fleming would have certainly known about it and he was possibly another source for Bond's gambling antics.

Popov was also a legendary ladies' man and was given the codename "Tricycle" for his fondness for taking two women to bed at the same time. In August 1941, while working as a German agent in the US, Popov discovered that the Japanese were preparing to attack Pearl Habor. He informed the FBI, but bureau-chief J. Edgar Hoover distrusted him. The information was not passed on and when Hoover learnt that Popov had taken a woman with him from New York to Florida he threatened him with arrest under the Mann Act unless he left the US immediately.

Later, when asked whether he was the inspiration for James Bond, Popov was dismissive.

"I doubt whether a flesh-and-blood Bond would last forty-eight hours as a spy," he said.

Fleming was fascinated by Stephenson's operation in New York and his secret Camp X in Canada which produced technical gadgets and forged documents. The laboratory there claimed to be able to reproduce the imprint of any typewriter. Fleming was enthralled.

He spent a few days there on a training course. Stephenson reckoned he was one of the best pupils the school ever had. Fleming particularly excelled in an exercise to plant a limpet mine to a derelict tanker moored in a lake. After a long swim at night, not unlike the one in *Live and Let Die*, Fleming affixed the mine and escaped undetected, one of the few trainees to do so. Stephen said Fleming was every bit as good as Bond in the water.

He also undertook weapons training with a variety of small arms and machine guns, along with courses on judo and self-defence. Fleming was the only one to pass Stephenson's initiative course. With the whole of the Toronto police force on alert, trainees were to plant imaginary bombs at key places around the city. Fleming's target was the power station. Donning his best suit, he simply rang the power-plant's managing director, explained that he was a visiting British engineer and arranged a meeting. Nevertheless, as a fully fledge agent, Fleming did not quite make the grade.

"The trouble was that although Ian was an outstanding trainee he just hadn't got the temperament for an agent or a genuine man of action," Stephenson said. "I'm not saying he lacked courage – he had a great deal. But he had far too much imagination."

At the end of the course, an instructor from the Shanghai police was booked in to a cheap hotel in Toronto. He had learnt to dodge bullets. Stephenson said it was a kind of circus trick – "if you fired at him from five yards he knew how to divert you sufficiently for the shot to go wide".

Trainees were given the name of the hotel and the room number. They would be told that a dangerous foreign agent was staying there who had to be killed. This was not an exercise. The idea was to find out whether they had the nerve to go through with a genuine killing. Stephenson briefed Fleming himself and made sure his gun was loaded.

"I told him that the games were over now and this was serious. 'Open that door, draw fast and shoot straight,' I told him. 'It'll be his life or yours.'"

Stephenson was watching when Fleming arrived. He got as far as the landing where he waited there for some time – then went away.

"He apologized about it afterwards," said Stephenson. "'You know,' he said, 'I just couldn't open that door. I couldn't kill a man that way.'"

However, Fleming did join Stephenson on a real-life mission. The Japanese consulate was on the floor below Stephenson's office in the Rockefeller Center. A cipher clerk there was sending coded radio messages back to Tokyo. Using duplicate keys, they broke into the consulate at three in the morning, microfilmed the code books and returned them to the safe. In *Casino Royale*, Bond says that he earned his double-O number after killing a cipher expert in the Rockefeller Center, though, in reality, the cipher clerk was left unharmed.

Stephenson lent another key ingredient to the Bond mix. According to Fleming, Stephenson mixed the largest dry martinis in America and served them in quart glasses. He was undoubtedly an influence. In a letter to the *Sunday Times* in 1962, Fleming said: "James Bond is a highly romanticized version of a true spy. The real thing is... William Stephenson."

Stephenson even had a plan to seize three millions dollars in gold belonging to the Vichy government held on the Caribbean island of Martinique which may have helped inspire *Goldfinger*. The plan never came to fruition.

In Washington, Fleming and Godfrey were given a curt tour of the FBI facilities – and the brush-off by Hoover. Nevertheless, Stephenson managed to arrange for Godfrey to have dinner with President Roosevelt and, soon after, Donovan was named Coordinator of Information. The COI also took an office New York's Rockefeller Center. It became the Office of Strategic Services the following year and, after the war, it became the CIA.

Of this trip and others they made, Godfrey said: "I could not have wished for a more agreeable companion than Ian Fleming on our many expeditions. I have never known him anything but buoyant, responsive and light-hearted, especially when things were going badly."

With his job done, Godfrey returned to England, leaving Fleming to help Donovan draw up what would become the charter for the OSS. To express his gratitude, Donovan gave Fleming a .38 Police Positive Colt, with inscription: "For Special Services." Fleming boasted that it had been given to him by the "father of the American Secret Service". Later he claimed that he had a hand in the creation of the CIA.

On his way home, Fleming stopped off in Spanish-occupied Tangiers, where he and the local Goldeneye agent H.L. Greenleaves got drunk and broke into a bullring where they marked out a twenty-foot V for victory in the sand. Greenleaves ended up in jail, temporarily, and Fleming had to apologize to his superior in Gibraltar.

"I am afraid you will have received something of a shock on hearing of my escapade with Greenleaves, of which I admit I was thoroughly ashamed," Fleming said, "but it appears to have created nothing but the most ribald mirth and so perhaps it was not as shameful as I thought it was."

Fleming attempted to get himself posted to Moscow, but was blocked by the head of the Military Mission there who had earlier dealings with Fleming and was not impressed. He wrote: "I know Fleming and from my experience of his activities in Germany before the war and of the reports he use to write I know him to be gullible and of poor and unbalanced judgement."

Instead, Fleming began working most closely with the Political Warfare Executive, making broadcasts in German telling the

Kriegsmarine their U-boats leaked. He also supplied debriefs of captured U-boat crews to Sefton Delmer, now head of PWE, who used the details in his black propaganda broadcasts put out on bogus German radio stations the PWE had set up. Also on the staff were Robert Harling, who Fleming knew from publishing circles before the war, and the thriller-writer Dennis Wheatley. He was also involved in an operation forging German documents.

Ever the gentleman, Fleming took captured German naval officers out for meals in fashionable restaurants in the hope of pumping them for information. They often got quite drunk. On one occasion a waiter called the police.

"It was only when back to the Admiralty, befuddled and no wiser," said Fleming, "that a furious Director of Naval Intelligence told us that the only result of our secret mission was to mobilize half of the narks of the Special Branch of Scotland Yard."

Fleming and his various girlfriends made the best of the privations of the war years. Although he complained that the Savoy were now making its martinis out of bath-tub gin and sherry, he could still get his Morland Specials, now emblazoned with three gold bands to denote his rank as commander. He increased his order to four hundred a week. Fleming went to great lengths to obtain other luxuries. His mistress, Ann O'Neill, said that Ian could stand anything except discomfort.

Fleming had assumed that the war was as good as over when the United States entered after Pearl Harbor in December 1941. He became rapidly disillusioned. When Singapore fell two months later, he blamed it on the fact that the British Army no longer shot deserters. Then he began to complain about Donovan – and even Stephenson.

Fleming's own contribution at that point was his involvement in Operation Postmaster. It was the idea of Captain Gus March-Phillips. He was a contemporary of Fleming – they had been born just two months apart. Both their fathers had been killed in 1917. Both were men of considerable charm and both liked fast cars. However, March-Phillips had done well at school and in officer training. Leaving the army, he became a successful novelist. In his 1938 novel *Ace High*, he created a protagonist called John Sprake who was a sportsman, card-player and a gambler – much like James Bond would turn out to be.

Rejoining the Army at the outbreak of World War II, he moved on to SOE initially as a training officer. Soon he persuaded the head of SOE Brigadier Colin McVean Gubbins – otherwise known as M – to set up a cross-Channel raiding force. He requisitioned a converted Brixham trawler – like the one used in *Goldfinger* – called the *Maid Honor*, and recruited a team of commanders who became known as the Maid Honor Force.

In 1941, reports came in that U-boats had refuelling bases in the rivers in the parts of West Africa controlled by Vichy France. SOE proposed to send the *Maid Honor* to find them. As this action required Admiralty approval, Fleming was called in as liaison officer. As the action was taking place in West Africa, the operatives were given the designation W, so March-Phillips became W.01, his second in command W.02, etc. They found no refuelling bases so, instead, they seized three enemy merchant vessels from neutral Spanish island of Fernando Po and sailed them to Lagos. The Germans condemned this as an act of piracy. Commander Fleming issued a communiqué saying: "In view of the German allegations that Allied naval forces have executed a cutting-out operation against Axis ships in the Spanish port of Santa Isabel, Fernando Po, the British Admiralty considers it necessary to state that no British or Allied ship was in the vicinity." It was not true, of course.

After March-Phillips returned to London and was debriefed by Fleming and others, he suggested setting up the Small Scale Raiding Force, a covert commando unit that would strike across the Channel, seizing German prisoners and other sources of intelligence. Soon after, Fleming – who was now signing himself in internal correspondence as just "F" – proposed to Admiral Godfrey a Naval Intelligence Commando Unit that would go in with any attacking force, head straight for any buildings that might contain intelligence documents and return directly with them.

Leading a cross-Channel raid in September 1942, March-Phillipps was killed. The three novels he published before the war drew on his own life and experiences, and there is speculation that, had he survived, John Sprake may well have become James Bond.

Chapter Six – Red Indians

Since the summer of 1941, Fleming had been studying the fall of Crete. While the island had been surrounded by the Royal Navy, German paratroopers had overwhelmed the 25,000 Commonwealth troops defending it. It was the first time a campaign had depended solely on airborne forces and British Naval Intelligence were keen to study the reasons for their defeat.

Fleming's interest focussed on one man – Obersturmbannführer Otto Skorzeny, who would later stage the daring raid to rescue Benito Mussolini from his mountain prison and become the inspiration behind Sir Hugo Drax in *Moonraker*. Fleming noticed that, while Skorzeny and his men had landed on Crete with the first wave, they did not take part in the main fighting. Instead they concentrated their efforts on overrunning the British headquarters, seizing maps, codes, orders and communications equipment before the defenders could destroy them. He asked divisional directors in the Admiralty, in such circumstances, what materials they would be looking for. Soon he had a shopping list. A unit of what Fleming called "Red Indians" was set up, operating out of Room 30 at the Admiralty. They were known officially as 30 Commando Unit, or 30 CU, later 30 Assault Unit, or 30 AU.

Unfortunately, the first action it took part in was the disastrous raid on Dieppe in August 1942. Again Fleming knew too much to risk losing him, but he was allowed to go along as an observer on board one of the ships. He took delight in seeing the casino on the front being destroyed by naval shell-fire. But when the Canadians were held up by withering fire and the attack began to go wrong, none of his men got ashore. His ship was then hit by shell-fire and was forced to return to England. Fleming used all his skill as a writer when he wrote up the raid for the department's Weekly Intelligence Report, putting as favourable a gloss on it as possible under the circumstances.

Godfrey and Fleming went to the US again to liaise with the now full-fledged OSS, though on the eve of their departure Godfrey was sacked as director of Naval Intelligence – or rather promoted out of office. In New York, at the 21 Club, Fleming was introduced to Walter Winchell, king of gossip journalists who had done much to stir up the Americans against the Nazis.

He moved on to Jamaica for an Anglo-American naval conference concerning the U-boats that were now sinking merchant shipping in the Caribbean, taking the train to Miami, as James Bond does with Solitaire in *Live and Let Die*. On Jamaica, Fleming stayed with his old school friend Ivar Bryce, now an SIS agent, in a house where Ian's hero Lord Nelson had stayed as a young man. On his flight back to Washington, Ian told Bryce: "When we have won this blasted war, I am going to live in Jamaica… and swim in the sea and write books."

Back in London, Fleming heard from his Goldeneye agents that the crews of three Italian miniature submarines had been captured, trying to attack British aircraft carriers in the harbour at Gibraltar. They had been delivered to Algeciras Bay by a tanker and deployed through a trap door in its hull. Fleming would use this idea in *Thunderball*. Indeed, in the book, Bond tells Felix Leiter of the CIA that their failure to spot was what going on in Algeciras Bay was "one of the blackest marks against Intelligence during the whole war".

Plans of the Anglo-American landings in Algeria and Morocco that November were now well advanced. Fleming's new intelligence force, 30 AU – under the cover name "Special Engineering Unit" – would go in with them. He took his men to Scotland Yard where an elderly chief inspector taught them the techniques of picking locks, breaking and entering, and safe blowing. Training session also involved the recognition and capture of ciphers, code books, intelligence reports, orders and new weapons and equipment. In Buckinghamshire, the commandoes were also put through their paces with plastic explosives, gelignite, booby traps, small-arms and minefield.

"At this stage, Ian was very excited," said Lieutenant Dunstan Curtis who led the raid. "You'd have thought he was going on the trip. It was an enormous adventure for him… He must have given an extraordinary amount of thought to this particular show. He had organized air pictures and maps and models to show us exactly where we would land and what to go for. He knew where the enemy HQ was. He told us what troops were there, what they were up to and what we ought to find."

They landed in American uniforms, but wearing British navy caps. Curtis carried a American M1 carbine and a Colt .45. Fleming himself carried a .25 Beretta throughout the war. This is the gun he gives to Bond until, in *Dr. No*, it is replaced by a Walther PPK.

Commandeering a French truck, Curtis and his men zigzagged across Algiers to the villa the Italians used as their naval headquarters. The Italians had no time to burn or bury their files. Fleming's men ransacked the place and code books, current Italian and German ciphers, the enemy's order of battle and a mass of other material was shipped back to Gibraltar, then on to London for analysis. They also managed to capture an *Abwehr* Enigma machine, which is not unlike the Spektor cipher machine Bond is sent to collect in *From Russia With Love*.

Fleming was also involved in Operation Mincemeat – the inspiration behind the book and film *The Man Who Never Was* – where a body was washed up on the shores of Spain carrying documents that indicated the next Allied landings would be in Greece and Sardinia, rather than Sicily where they actually took place. Outlines of the plan had appeared in a memo Fleming had circulated in September 1939. 30 AU also landed in Sicily, again capturing a large amount of documents.

Fleming crossed the Atlantic twice more to attend summits between Churchill and Roosevelt. On one occasion he ran Peter, who had been posted to India and was then angling to run all deception operations in the Pacific. During the Quebec Conference of August 1943, Fleming took the opportunity to visit Camp X again. He also attended the Churchill–Roosevelt conference in Cairo, travelling with Joan Bright, a women he had got a job for at SIS and had been seeing for about a year.

In the run-up to D-Day, Fleming liaised with Lieutenant Alan Schneider of US Naval Intelligence who helped out when Fleming got involved with an attractive captain in the US Women's Army Corps. Fleming explained: "Women are like pets, like dogs; men are the only real human beings you could be friends with." However, when a long-term girlfriend who he had treated abominably was killed in an air-raid and he was called to identify the body, Fleming was visibly shaken and carried her bracelet on his key ring.

Before D-Day, Fleming was running a special committee channelling information from Bletchley Park to those who needed it. He also paid a visit to 30 AU in North Africa and took a shooting trip to the Atlas Mountains with the British minister Duff Cooper. His "Red Indians" had now swelled to three hundred, with a core of trained intelligence officers and a large force of Royal Marines to protect them. Back in England, Fleming compiled a list of German equipment he wanted them to capture. Their maps were marked with crosses where V-1 launch sights were being installed in the Pas de Calais, along with harbours, airfields and factories where secret weapons might be held. Then a week before D-Day, he held a dinner at the Gargoyle Club for the unit's officers and their wives and girlfriends.

Landing at Arromanches, 30 AU captured a German radar station intact and Dunstan Curtis, armed with Fleming's shopping list, began shipping equipment back to him. Despite their successes, 30 Assault Unit had a bad reputation when it came to drink and women, prompting Admiral Cunningham to call them 30 Indecent Assault Unit. When their well-tailored commander crossed the Channel to tell them off, they did not take it kindly, especially when he told them that some brandy they had captured was undrinkable, so they deliberately put him in the way of German fire. Fleming was not popular with General Patton, who was in overall command of that sector, either. He did not like sailors, especially those who rode around in jeeps on dry land. After inspecting the vast V-2 installations the Allies had uncovered – another inspiration for *Moonraker* – Fleming was invited to have lunch with Patton. He ducked out. Instead he went for a picnic with Robert Harling who asked him what he was going to do after the war.

"Why, write the spy story to end all spy stories," said Fleming.

"I almost choked on my Spam," recalled Harling.

To avoid trouble with Patton, 30 AU attached itself to the Free French for the liberation of Paris, where they took over the German Navy headquarters in the Rothschild mansion, making another haul of documents. The only real damage was done when one member of the troop followed Fleming's instructions of how to blow a safe with gelgnite.

Fleming extended his shopping list. It now included an expert on liquid oxygen who was found at the address he provided and a secret store of acoustic homing torpedoes years ahead of anything the Allies had. This too was uncovered.

He was back in London, visiting Ann at the home of her other lover Esmond Harmsworth, now Lord Rothermere, when a telegram arrived telling her that her husband, Lord O'Neill had been killed in Italy. Ian was uncharacteristically sympathetic and thoughtfully handled the practicalities concerning their children.

Fleming volunteered to inspect the intelligence infrastructure of the British Pacific Fleet which was now taking on the remnants of the Japanese navy. In Colombo, he met a Wren named Clare Blanshard and told her that he never intended to spend another winter in England. He was smitten and she went on to be Kemsley representative in New York when he worked for the company. Fleming travelled on to Australia, then returned to England by way of Pearl Habor.

By this time, 30 AU were entering Germany. Fleming gave a new list of German inventions he wanted to get his hands on. These included a jet-powered hydrofoil and "Cleopatra", an amphibious device that exploded beach defences. Another item on the list was a one-man submarine. Admiral Ramsay, now in overall command, said he doubted that such a thing existed, so the midget submarine 30 AU had found was put on a tank transporter and sent round to him.

"The thing's a toy," said Ramsay. But when he looked down the periscope, he could see the eye of a dead German who had drowned when the mini-sub had foundered.

The men of 30 AU captured a boat designed to run on hydrogen peroxide developed at the submarine works in Hamburg, the torpedo experimental station at Eckernforder and the entire German Navy's Warfare Science Department. Fleming went personally to seize the German Naval archives which dated back to 1870. They were shipped back to London, along with an elderly admiral to edit them. Flemings final signal to his Red Indians was: "Find immediately the twelve top German naval commanders and make each one write ten thousand words on why Germany lost the war."

At a party celebrating the closing of Sefton Delmer's black-propaganda radio stations, Ian was seen doodling on Admiralty blotting paper. Asked what he was drawing, he said it was the house he would live in on Jamaica. He also talked about the book he was going to write. He told a colleague writing it would be just like making salad dressing – all you needed were the right ingredients in the right quantities.

Some of the ingredients were already to hand. One evening in a pub in Westminster in 1943, Fleming had been introduced C.H. Forster from the Ministry of Aircraft Production when the conversation turned to call-up numbers. Forster said that he had initially been a "Bevin Boy". Conscripted to work in the mines, he had been given the designation DMZ 7 by the Ministry of Labour.

"Another gentleman nearby agreed that it could not be a War Department number," said Forster. "That would have had eight digits, such as 10,000,007, which a telephone operator would describe as one oh treble oh double oh seven."

Fleming said he liked the sound of that asked if he could use it for a book he was writing.

"I agreed that he could," said Forster, "especially as 007 had no traceable value, but sounded impressive and secretive. I also asked how he invented names of this characters."

"That's easy," said Fleming. "I take the first couple of names from my house at school and swap their Christian names."

"In my case, they were James Aitken and Harry Bond," said Forster. "So you would have Harry Aitken and James Bond. Fleming's face lit up. James Bond 007 was born."

During a stroll in Hyde Park in 1945, the widowed Ann O'Neill told him that she was going to marry Lord Rothermere. Fleming appeared unperturbed, but he would not give her up. He would always be on hand, taking a new flat just around the corner from their house in Montagu Square. There were other women, of course, but his affair with Ann continued while he maintained Lord Rothermere as a friend.

For Ann, a clandestine affair while being married to another man added extra spice to their relationship. In 1947, after a few days together she wrote: "It was so short and so full of happiness, and I am afraid I loved cooking for you and sleeping beside you and being whipped by you… I don't think I have ever loved like this before."

In reply, Fleming could, for once, write from the heart: "All the love I have for you has grown out of me because you made it grow. Without you I would still be hard and dead and cold and quite unable to write this childish letter, full of love and jealousies and adolescence."

Chapter Seven – Goldeneye

After the war, Lord Kemsley offered Fleming a generous salary to be the foreign manager of his newspaper group. He could have been made foreigner editor, but did not want the responsibility. Kemsley allowed him two-months' holiday a year. So, by the end of 1945, Fleming was on his way to Jamaica to start building his new house on a plot Ivar Bryce had found for him on the north coast. It was near the town of Oracabessas – "Golden Head" in Spanish – which would make an appearance in *Live and Let Die*. The house would be called Goldeneye, after the wartime operation. There he would swim among the brightly coloured fishes and spear lobster for dinner.

The newly knighted Sir William Stephenson also moved to the island. He introduced Fleming to another resident – Lord Beaverbrook, the owner of the *Daily Express*. Fleming also struck up a friendship with neighbours Tommy and Marion Leiter, who lent their surname to Bond's CIA sidekick.

When they first met, Marion Leiter chastised Fleming for his treatment of her friend Millicent Rogers.

"Mr Fleming," she said. "I consider you a cad."

"You're quite right," he replied, unrepentant. "Shall we have a drink on it?"

Sailing back to England on the liner *Queen Mary* the following spring, Fleming was introduced to Winston Churchill, who made it plain that he would rather have met Peter than Ian.

In his office at the *Sunday Times*, Fleming installed a large map of the world with flashing lights showing the whereabouts of Kemsley's some eighty foreign correspondents. Others found his love of gadgetry faintly ludicrous. Many of the correspondents he took on were spies, or former spies. Some of the reports they sent back were often not for publication and were passed on to the intelligence services. One Far East correspondent, a hard-drinking Australian named Richard Hughes, was a double agent for the SIS, after the KGB had approached him. Otherwise, reporters were told to give their stories "brightness and champagne" to cheer up a Britain that was undergoing a period of drab austerity while it was being rebuilt after the war.

When Ann took off to New York on the *Queen Elizabeth* with her new husband, Fleming grew jealous. Learning that Rothermere was travelling on to Canada alone, he flew over to New York to catch up with Ann in the Plaza Hotel. She begged him to go, saying she now had a ladies' maid.

"Get rid of the bitch," said Fleming. She did as she was told and he stayed four nights.

During the trip, he suffered pains in the chest and consulted a heart specialist, whose diagnosis was: "The patient admits to smoking seventy cigarettes a day and drinking at least a quarter of a bottle of gin. He is not seriously ill but during the last two months has complained of a constricting pain in the heart. He has slightly low blood pressure, the cardiograph shows an inverted T wave, but there are not important symptoms of heart weakness. The above symptoms could all be the result of nicotine poisoning. I instructed the patient that the situation could not be improved by medication – only by will power."

The medical report is reminiscent of that on Bond at the beginning of *Thunderball*. It also seriously underestimated Fleming's intake of alcohol. He liked to start the evening with large martini's which were virtually iced gin. Later, he switched to vodka. He and Ivar Bryce came up with a cocktail they called the Vesper, which they drank at six in the evening, the time of vespers. It consisted of three measures of Gordon's gin, one of vodka and half a measure of Kina Lillet. He gave the recipe in *Casino Royale*, but gave the name Vesper to the book's heroine.

On other occasions Fleming was seen to be bruised and hinted at a sado-masochistic element to his relationship with Ann. "All this damage has to be paid for some time," he warned. And so it was.

"I long for you to whip me because I love being hurt by you and kissed afterwards," Ann wrote to him. "It's very lonely not to be beaten and shouted at every five minutes."

It has often been remarked that there is an element of sadism in the Bond novels.

On Jamaica, Goldeneye began to take shape. It was stark concrete construction, reminiscence of a district commissioner's residence at the height of Empire. Noël Coward, later a neighbour, once referred to it as the "Golden eye, nose and throat clinic", though wrote a song about his stay there. When Ann first visited, she was appalled by the Spartan accommodation, the lack of baths and the absence of windowpanes – only slatted louvers as Fleming liked gentle tropical breezes wafting through the house. An amateur naturalist, she brought with her a *Field Guide to the Birds of the West Indies*. It was written by an American academic named James Bond.

After Ann left, Fleming went shark hunting, dragging the carcases of a cow and a donkey out to sea as bait. He said it was the most thrilling thing he had done in his life and provided the climax for *Live and Let Die*.

Fleming took on staff, including a housekeeper who stayed on at Goldeneye for the next seventeen years. Other friends visited. They swam naked in the warm sea and Fleming was full of stories of diving on the reef there. Evenings were spent partying with other denizens of the up-market north shore, where everyone seemed to know about his relationship with Lady Rothermere. Fleming wrote a piece about north-shore society for *Horizon* magazine, edited by his friend Cyril Connolly.

In London, Fleming mixed with other literary luminaries such as Osbert and Edith Sitwell, T.S. Eliot, biographer Peter Quennell and the academic Maurice Bowra, along with William Plomer who later edited some of the Bond novels.

In London, Fleming also took on a succession of pretty au pairs, though he would spend his evenings at Boodle's or dining innocently with the Rothermeres. But whenever Harmsworth was away at the office, Fleming found himself in Ann's bedroom. Meanwhile he continued his search for his perfect woman who, he said, was "thirtyish, Jewish, a companion who would not need an education… would aim to please, have firm flesh and kind eyes".

In 1948, Ann fell pregnant and miscarried. Her husband stayed at her bedside, though it was generally assumed that the child was Fleming's. She said that his thoughtful letters at this troubled time convinced her that she loved him. In reply, she urged him to write the book he was always talking about. At the time, he had dreamed up a crime story where the murder weapon was a frozen leg of lamb which was disposed of by being cooked and eaten. Roald Dahl, who knew Fleming from the war, used the idea in his 1952 story "Lamb to the Slaughter".

After the miscarriage, there was no hiding Fleming's relationship with Ann. Lord Kemsley duly upbraided his foreign manager on his ungentlemanly behaviour. But the affair continued with Fleming and the Rothermere still mixing in the same social circles.

The next time Fleming went to Jamaica, Ann went with him, though to keep up appearances she said she was staying with Noël Coward. On her return to England, Ann got an ultimatum from Rothermere – she must stop seeing Fleming or he would divorce her. Nevertheless, in the summer of 1949, Ian and Ann rented a cottage near Royal St George's golf club in Kent from thriller writer Eric Ambler.

Fleming's health began to falter. Doctors again advised he cut down on his drinking. That Christmas he went alone to Jamaica while Ann threw herself into the social whirl on the Continent, though she wrote saying she missed Ian and whipping him.

Fleming still enjoyed the good things in life, despite austerity. While at the *Sunday Times*, he continued to lunch at his club and, with Britain gradually coming off rationing, he introduced the food columnist of an American magazine to the *Daily Graphic*. He got his friend Stephen Potter's book *Gamesmanship* reviewed by the *Sunday Times*, but rejected Fitzroy Maclean's book *Eastern Approaches* for serialization. Fleming also became a director of Dropmore Press, a Kemsley subsidiary, and worked as a commissioning editor. One of the company's titles was *Book Handbook*, aimed at fellow bibliophiles.

The devaluation of the pound in 1949 hit Kemsley's foreign news operation. It was also noted that Fleming's idea of foreign news came from lifestyle magazines such as *Life* and *Paris Match*, rather than *The New York Times* or *Le Monde*. At the height of the Cold War, he strove to obtain a visa for a *Sunday Times* correspondent in Moscow – the only one from any Commonwealth newspaper – then sent wine writer and connoisseur Cyril Ray. He also started a magazine on typography and design, set a literary competition for the *Spectator* and wrote a speech for Princess – soon to be Queen – Elizabeth to give to the American press. It was not used. Meanwhile he kept up his contacts with SIS.

Ian and Ann Ian took a flat in the block in Chelsea where T.S. Eliot lived. Every July he did two weeks naval training, allowing him to retain his rank of commander in the RNVR. In the summer of 1950, he went to stay with Ivar Bryce who then had a house in Vermont. He would visit New England nearly every summer and scenes from the short story "For Your Eyes Only" and the novel *The Spy Who Loved Me* would be set there.

The following spring, having just finished a nine-year affair with Cecil Day-Lewis, the writer Rosamond Lehmann arrived at Goldeneye, aiming to bed Ian. But Ann was there and she had to be palmed off on Noël Coward – a disappointment for both of them.

By the summer of 1951, Ann was pregnant again. Rothermere divorced her. Ann and Ian decided to marry and her £100,000 settlement set them up for best part of ten years. Friends and family were aghast. They did not believe that Ian was the marrying type and thought Ann had become pregnant to ensnare him.

In Jamaica, where they intended to marry, Ian, finally, began to write the thriller he had been talking about for nearly ten years. For three hours in the morning he pounded his twenty-year-old Imperial portable typewriter. After an afternoon nap, he would read through what he had written and amend it. It was a routine he would follow during his stays at Goldeneye over the next twelve years.

Chapter Eight – The Birth of Bond

Fleming's biographer John Pearson says that James Bond was born on the morning of 15 January 1952. However, Ann later said that Ian only started writing the first Bond book, *Casino Royale*, after dining with Noël Coward, who arrived in Jamaica on 16 February and urged him to get on with it. The book was finished on 18 March. This would mean that he finished the 62,000-word novel in just four weeks, at the astonishing speed of over two thousand words a day, particularly as he had no notes. Just a name – James Bond.

"I wanted the simplest, dullest, plainest-sounding name I could find," he said. "James Bond seemed perfect."

Fleming said he wrote *Casino Royale* to take his mind off his forthcoming marriage. It was a farewell to his bachelor days. This annoyed Ann, particularly as the last words of the novel are: "The bitch is dead now." However, it was perfectly timed. Spying was very much in the news then with the defection of the Cambridge spies, Guy Burgess and Donald Maclean.

Sibling rivalry might also have had a hand. That year, Peter Fleming published *The Sixth Column*, a novel set in the secret service with a Bond-style hero named Colonel Hackforth. The book was dedicated to Ian. Fleming also needed money to help towards the upkeep of the extravagant ex-wife of a millionaire press baron and their forthcoming child. It was also a way to divert his energies.

Ann was not about to risk losing a second child, so she banned sex. However, she was there to give him the support he needed to get down to work.

They married just six days after *Casino Royale* was finished. The nuptials were toasted with dry martini's at Noël Coward's house. They honeymooned in Nassau and New York.

Back in London, Fleming had to live, not only with his spend-thrift wife Ann, but also with her two children from her first marriage, plus a parrot called Jackie. While making his contribution to the support of this menagerie, he bought himself a reward for finishing the novel – a gold-plated Royal typewriter which he had shipped over from America. In future, he said, he would write on vellum studded with diamonds, using his own blood as ink. Clearly he was proud of himself. But it was not until 12 May that he told his friend William Plomer, then a literary adviser at Jonathan Cape, that he had written a book. He promised to send him the manuscript, but two months later Plomer had to remind him. Fleming then sent it reluctantly, saying that he was intending to make revisions on his return to Jamaica. Nevertheless Plomer sent it to a fellow reader at Cape who also liked it. Jonathan Cape himself rejected it, but was persuaded to publish it when Peter Fleming put in a good word for his brother.

Meanwhile Kemsley relaunched the *Book Handbook* as the quarterly *Book Collector* and made Fleming a director of his new imprint, Queen Anne Press, where he published offerings from Evelyn Waugh and Cyril Connolly.

On 12 August, Ann gave birth to their son, Caspar, by Caesarean section. Fleming was seen to weep openly. While Ann was in hospital, he started the final revision of *Casino Royale* on his gold typewriter, though afterwards reverted to his Imperial portable. He also wrote an article on Jamaica for the *Spectator*. A piece he wrote on road safety was rejected by the *Sunday Times*, but later appeared in the *Daily Graphic* under the pen name Frank Gray, thanks to the good offices of Lord Kemsley.

Fleming did not have a literary agent so he negotiated his own deal with Cape, assigning the book rights to Glidrose Productions, a small company he owned, to ease any tax burden. Friends helped him find a publisher in the US and author Paul Gallico put Fleming in touch with his agent in Hollywood.

Fleming was repelled by the scar left by Ann's Caesarean, ending their sex life. He also avoided her friends who looked down in his literary efforts. Even so, the following January, they flew to New York to research *Live and Let Die*, travelling by train from Penn Station to Florida as in the book. In St Petersburg, he checked out the waterfront for a suitable site for Ourobouros Worm and Bait Shippers, Inc, a front for Mr Big. Then they flew on to Jamaica, where Cabarita Island, near Oracabessa, became Mr Big's hideaway the Isle of Surprise. The sections on voodoo were gleaned from Ann's friend Paddy Leigh Fermor's book *The Traveller's Tree*, which was written, in part, at Goldeneye. Fleming also witnessed a voodoo funeral in Jamaica.

Guests at Goldeneye that winter included Graham Greene, novelist Angus Wilson, painter Lucian Freud and actress Katherine Hepburn. Meanwhile, news came from the nanny in London of Caspar's first tooth.

Chapter Nine – Becoming a Bestseller

Back in London, Fleming met aqua-lung pioneer Jacques Cousteau who invited him to a dive in the Mediterranean, so he was away when *Casino Royale* was published on 13 April 1953. Ann stayed in Antibes with Somerset Maugham who praised the book. For the rest of his life, Fleming kept a copy of *The Times Literary Supplement* which contained a glowing review by Alan Ross, a literary friend of Ann's.

Fleming was well connected. He could depend on reviews in the papers owned by Kemsley and Beaverbrook, though he received cool notices from Rothermere's publications. Family friends owned leading booksellers W.H. Smith, which also helped. Fleming had designed his own book jacket and flyers, and constantly pushed Cape over promotion. This paid off and the first print run of 4,750 sold out. Soon Hollywood was showing an interest.

Fleming used the success of the second and third print runs to renegotiate the contract and up his royalty. In New York he signed a deal with Macmillan, where the editor cut much of the sex and violence. But Fleming was more concerned with promotion. Returning on the *Queen Elizabeth*, he corrected the proofs of *Live and Let Die*. When these were circulated to film companies and attracted praise, he decided that his next book would be written specifically with a movie in mind. That winter, he began *Moonraker*.

He found ways to fund his research, ostensibly by providing articles for Kemsley newspapers. Later he took over the Atticus column in the *Sunday Times*. Those he wrote about did him favours. He also used Atticus to attack Senator Joe McCarthy's witch-hunt of Communist sympathizers in America. After all, it was James Bond, not Joe McCarthy, who was the ultimate Cold Warrior.

Fleming consulted old intelligence colleagues for information about V2-style rockets and the Nazi Werewolves who were supposed to fight on after the war, both of which make an appearance in *Moonraker*. The megalomaniac traits of the book's villain Hugo Drax were gleaned from a Harley Street psychiatrist.

Live and Let Die also got good reviews in the UK, but *Casino Royale* was given a cool reception in the US and *Moonraker* failed to attract a movie offer. Nevertheless Fleming was determined to continue with the series.

While writing *Moonraker* Fleming had begun to think more deeply about James Bond. It was clear he was creating a series of fantastic adventures about the same central character. But, he realized, it did not matter how fantastic the stories were as long as the author believed in the fantasy. Then the reader would believe it too.

The production of the Bond books had already fallen into a pattern. The first three months of the year were spent writing the manuscript of the next book in Jamaica. Then he returned to London to prepare the book he had written the year before for publication. Meanwhile, the book he had written the year before that came out in the US. The rest of the year, Fleming used his position at the *Sunday Times* to research exotic locations. He paid great attention to detail, even driving the routes Bond takes in the books. After failing to reach Arthur C. Clarke who was away in the US at the time, he got experts from the British Interplanetary Society to look over the details of the rocketry in *Moonraker*.

He visited London's Hatton Garden to research *Diamonds Are Forever* and discussed the problems of diamond smuggling with Sir Percy Sillitoe, formerly head of MI5, then head of security at De Beers. William Stephenson had sent him an article about Saratoga Springs in upstate New York for background. Fleming headed there and, by mistake, happened upon a rundown mud bath – which became the Acme Mud and Sulphur Baths Bond visits to pay off the jockey who then gets bumped off. A friend he met there had a Studillac – a Studebaker with a Cadillac engine. This also appeared in the book.

Ever the business man, Fleming signed up to become European controller of the North American Newspaper Alliance (NANA), a new features agency owed by Bryce. This allowed him to negotiation lucrative syndication deals with Kemsley and Beaverbrook's Express newspapers.

Back in London, Fleming avoided Ann's friends – who now included biographer James Pope-Hennessy and celebrity photographer Cecil Beaton – finding them rather stuck up. One night he returned from his club to find them laughing at a reading of one of his sex scenes.

Leaving Ann in London, he took the *Queen Elizabeth* to New York, then went on to Los Angeles by train. On the way, he taught the steward how to mix his martinis. In LA, he sold a movie option on *Casino Royale* for $600. Curtis Brown, the agent he had taken on in New York, sold the TV rights and a hour-long version of the book appeared on CBS's Chrysler Climax Mystery Theater in 1954 – Bond's first outing on screen. Some liberties were taken with the plotline though. Bond was an American agent, while Leiter became British. Money was also offered for options on *Live and Let Die*, *Moonraker* and subsequent Bond books, but Fleming thought he could get more and turned them down.

Fleming visited the LA Police Department, where he was briefed on the surveillance techniques that greeted Bond when he arrived at Las Vegas in *Diamonds Are Forever*. Then he flew to Las Vegas with Ernie Cuneo, an associate of Bryce's who had been Donovan's liaison with BSC during the war. Fleming was delighted to find the slot machine in the airport that gave two-minutes of oxygen for 25 cents. This, again, Bond used in the book. Cuneo took Fleming on a tour of the casinos in Las Vegas. Making small bets, they quit when they were $1 ahead, then drank a glass of champagne and moved on. By the end of the evening they could boast that they had beaten every casino in town. In the book, Ernie Cuneo appeared as Ernest Cureo, Bond's cab driver and undercover Pinkerton man in Nevada.

While writing *Diamonds Are Forever* in Jamaica that winter, Fleming became across a local character called Red Grant, famed for his "hot bak soup" – a concoction of langoustines and exotic roots.

Fleming used his name for the assassin in *From Russian With Love*. Evelyn Waugh was also on hand to help him polish up the love scenes.

"The author must be in a state of lustful excitement when writing of love," he said.

Live and Let Die sold poorly in the US despite an endorsement from the American master of crime fiction Raymond Chandler who Fleming had met at a party in London thrown by the poet Stephen Spender. However, the $600 movie option on *Casino Royale* turned into $6,000 for the rights. Fleming blew the money a Ford Thunderbird, which Ann hated. He loved the car so much, Ann nicknamed him Thunderbird – or, more cruelly, T.B.

Bond spoofs began to appear. The first was from a reader at Cape. The second, from the colleague of Atticus, was published in the Christmas issue of the *Spectator*. Fleming was delighted. Then Fleming's friend Billy Woodward, who used to accompany him to the racing at Saratoga, was shot and killed in a case that became a *cause célèbre*. As a result, *Diamonds Are Forever* was dedicated to J.F.C.B – Ivar Bryce – "E.L.C." – Ernie Cureo – "and W.W. Jr" – Woodward – "at Saratoga 1954 and '55".

That September Fleming accompanied Scotland Yard's assistant commissioner Sir Ronald Howe – who appeared as Superintendent Ronnie Vallace in *Moonraker* – to the Interpol Conference in Istanbul, hoping to get an insight into international crime. Instead, the trip gave him an interesting setting for his next Bond adventure, *From Russia With Love*. He was shown around the city by an outgoing, Oxford-educated Turk named Nazim Kalkavan, who boasted of drinking, smoking and making love too much. He became the model for Darko Karim, the Istanbul SIS station chief who assisted Bond. Fleming returned on the Simplon-Orient Express where Bond bedded Tatiana Romanova and fought it out with Red Grant.

When Queen Anne Press found itself in financial difficulties, Fleming bought the *Book Collector*, which gave him some of the academic credibility he craved. The rest of the company was bought by Robert Maxwell – a possible model for any number of Bond villains – though Fleming remained a director until his death.

Through a friend from Eton, Fleming became a member of the Royal College of Art and, with Ann, he visited Anthony Eden at the prime minister's country retreat, Chequers. They were told not to mention runaway spies Burgess and Maclean.

Returning to the US to sell NANA at a welcome profit, he noted that the American public were at last taking notice of Bond, perhaps because Pocket Book's dime-store edition of *Casino Royale* – retitled *You Asked For It* – had the picture of a girl in a low-cut, strapless dress on the cover.

The American critics were a little kinder with *Moonraker*.

"I don't know anyone who writes about gambling more vividly than Fleming," said *The New York Times*.

Hollywood offered $1,000 for a nine-month movie option. Meanwhile, Cape accepted £5,000 from Rank – who owned

Pinewood Studios, Bond's eventual home – leaving Fleming to unmake the Hollywood deal.

"I don't mind in the least getting in bad with Hollywood," he said. "If they ever want one of by books, you can bet they'll buy it even if I'm Jack the Ripper."

Meanwhile Rank had no idea of what to do with *Moonraker*. Though he had started it with a movie in mind, Fleming was well aware of the problem.

"The reason it breaks so badly in half as a book," he said, "is because I had to more or less grafted the first half of the book onto my film idea in order to bring it up to the necessary length."

He proposed a short biography of Marthe Richard, who spied for France as a prostitute in World War I and as brothel-keeper in World War II. After the war, she became a politician and introduced the law that closed the brothels down. It was known as *La Loi de Marthe Richard*, which is one of the plot points in *Casino Royal*. However, Curtis Brown persuaded Fleming to stick to fictional spies.

In *From Russia With Love*, Bond reads *The Mask of Dimitrios* by Eric Ambler, a classic thriller set in Istanbul. Fleming himself had read the book for local colour. Many now saw him as Ambler's heir and Ambler put him in touch with accountants and lawyers who created tax shelters for the money that was now flooding in from James Bond. Bond books were then appearing in foreign languages and the foreign rights manager at Curtis Brown, Peter Janson-Smith, quit to become Fleming's agent.

On his way to Jamaica to work on *From Russia With Love*, Fleming met Truman Capote, who had written a fictional account of the Woodward murder called *Answered Prayer*. He amused Fleming with tales of his recent trip to Russia and came to stay at Goldeneye. This amused Ann who declared Goldeneye to be the last heterosexual household in a growing gay enclave. Meanwhile, Richard Hughes, at Fleming's urging, secured the first interview with Burgess and Maclean in Moscow.

Alone in Jamaica that winter, Fleming met Blanche Blackwell, a wealthy divorcee who lived nearby. When they were introduced, he asked if she was a lesbian. She later said she thought he was the rudest man she had ever met, but was physically attracted to him and invited him to her house for drinks. Afterwards, they swam together at Goldeneye. She was the dark-haired Jewess of his dreams and is thought to have been the model for Pussy Galore in *Goldfinger*. While he mentioned Blanche in his letters to Ann, he put her off the scent by writing mainly about the time he spent with Noël Coward and other homosexual friends.

While in Nassau to write a piece for the *Sunday Times*, Fleming visited the flamingo sanctuary on the island of Inagua – which became Dr. No's hideaway, Crab Key. A naturalist from the Audubon Society briefed him on guano, the cormorant dung used for fertilizer that was the source of Dr. No's wealth. They even travelled around the island on a strange swamp-buggy, the inspiration for Dr. No's fire-breathing monster.

Diamonds Are Forever got good reviews. Fleming was particularly pleased with the one Raymond Chandler wrote for the *Sunday Times*. The creator of Philip Marlowe said he loved it when James Bond was "exposing himself unarmed to half a dozen thin-lipped killers, and neatly dumping them into a heap of fractured bones".

In private, Fleming wrote to Chandler: "If one has a grain of intelligence it is difficult to go on being serious about a character like James Bond. You after all write 'novels of suspense' – if not sociological studies – whereas my books are straight pillow fantasies of the bang-bang, kiss-kiss variety." When Chandler died in 1959, Fleming published their letters in the *London Magazine*.

Fleming also admitted that he did not take his books seriously enough because he had meekly accepted "having my head ragged off about them in family circles". He got his own back though. Arthur "Boofy" Gore, later the Earl of Arran and a relative by marriage, objected to his nickname appearing in *Diamonds Are Forever*, particularly as Leiter says: "Kidd's a pretty boy. His friends call him 'Boofy'. Probably shacks up with Wint. Some of these homos make the worst killers."

Suffering from sciatica, Fleming took himself off to Enton Hall, a "naturopathic" health farm which he satirized in *Thunderball*. Promising to give Ann a holiday, he took her to the next Interpol Conference in Vienna. Visiting Berlin on the way, they met up with Antony and Rachel Terry, two old friends from his Naval Intelligence days who told him about Emma Wolff, an ugly NKVD agent with dyed red hair. Wolff became the model for Rosa Klebb in *From Russia With Love*.

Returning to London, Fleming was suffering with kidney stones – only morphine would still the pain. He consoled himself with the idea that F. Scott Fitzgerald was dead at forty-four. Fleming was already forty-eight. But he complained to Chandler that he was getting fed up with Bond. *Diamonds Are Forever* had stretched his literary powers to their limits. He had nothing more to give.

Seeking new thrills, Fleming began playing bridge for higher stakes. He visited Ivar Bryce in Nassau to gamble in the casinos, and set the short story "Quantum of Solace" there. In the Bahamas he met former Harvard football star, John "Shipwreck" Sims Kelly, who knew everyone from the Duke of Windsor to Ernest Hemingway and introduced Ian to Aristotle Onassis, another in the Bond-villain mould.

Ian also spent time at Ivar Bryce's other home-from-home, Schloss Mittersill, a sports club for the super-rich near Kitzbühel. During the war, the Nazis had used it for pseudo-scientific studies of the Asiatic races and it became the model for Piz Gloria, Ernst Blofeld's alpine research facility in *On Her Majesty's Secret Service*.

At this louche establishment, Fleming indulged his passion for women and black lingerie. He also met the wife of Prince Alex Hohenlohe, former showgirl Patricia Wilder, there. She was known universally as Honeychile and he used the name Honeychile Wilder for the heroine of his next book, *Dr. No*.

Back in England, Ann began an affair with Labour Party leader Hugh Gaitskell. While she tried to promote Gaitskell with Beaverbrook, Fleming was paying court to the press baron's granddaughter, Lady Jeanne Campbell, in New York.

Fleming wrote the pilot for a TV series starring American secret agent Commander James Gunn. The villain would be the Chinese-German Dr. No who lived on a Caribbean island near an Anglo-American missile testing range. A part was written in for Ian's friend the Jamaican swimming champion Barrington Roper. The project came to nothing, but the Roper character reappeared in the book *Dr. No*.

A Glaswegian gun enthusiast named Geoffrey Boothroyd wrote complaining that the .25 Beretta Bond used was a "ladies' gun" and recommended a .38 Smith & Wesson Centennial Airweight carried in a Berns Martin Triple-draw holster. These sentiments appear in the mouth of Major Boothroyd, the departmental armourer in *Dr. No*, though they settle on a Walther PPK. Meanwhile, it was noted that Fleming had begun turning up the collar of his overcoat, perhaps to look more like Bond.

Delighted with manuscript for *From Russian With Love*, Macmillan began promoting *Diamonds Are Forever* in the US. After reading *Live and Let Die*, CIA chief Richard Helms contacted the head of MI5, Roger Hollis, and asked about Fleming. Hollis claimed never to have heard of him. However, Fleming was soon to come to the attention of the security services after Anthony Eden resigned due to "ill health" after the Suez crisis and went to Goldeneye to recuperate. Blanche was on hand to supervise arrangements. When this came to Ann's ears, she assumed that she and Ian were having an affair. Blanche now had no reason to resist. Unperturbed, Fleming stole the story from his failed TV pilot and was getting on with *Dr. No*.

Fleming was in Tangiers interviewing a real-life spy about a diamond scam for the *Sunday Times* when *From Russia With Love* came out. His publishers were now claiming that Fleming had sold over a million books in English and was translated into a dozen other languages. But after his murderous run-in with Rosa Klebb on the last page of the book, several reviews concluded they had seen the last of James Bond and were surprised when he was resurrected in *Dr. No*.

The *Daily Express* began publishing *Casino Royale* as a cartoon strip, despite Flemings' misgivings. He also published a non-fiction account of the diamond scam he had investigated in Tangiers as *The Diamond Smugglers* and Rank made an offer on the film rights. This alienated his brother-in-law Hugo Charteris whose *Picnic at Porokorro* covered the same ground. By then Flemings' marriage had broken down to the point where he was seen making drunken lunges at women at parties.

He planned another non-fiction book off the back of a proposed series of articles for the *Sunday Times* called, tentatively, "Round the World in Eight Adventures". Meanwhile, he returned to Goldeneye – and Blanche – to write *Goldfinger*.

Returning to England, Fleming began playing golf with Blanche's brother, John Blackwell, who provided technical details for the match Bond plays against Auric Goldfinger. The short, tight sixth known as "The Maiden" where they played at Sandwich became "The Virgin" in the book. Blackwell got a name-check in the book as a big-time drug dealer. Another crucial name-check proved more crucial. Blackwell's cousin was married to the architect Erno Goldfinger. When the book was published and he threatened to sue, Fleming suggested inserting an erratum slip changing the name to "Goldprick" throughout.

While James Bond was now proving a hit with the public, the critics sharpened their knives, accusing *Dr. No* of everything from snobbery and sadism to product placement. Chandler gave the book a good review in the *Sunday Times*, but then the wheels had been greased as Fleming had already commissioned him to interview Lucky Luciano on Capri, all expenses paid.

Ducking the brickbats that were soon flying in the US too, Fleming headed to the Seychelles for the first of his globe-trotting "Eight Adventures". He set the short story "The Hildebrand Rarity" there and his article helped the Seychelles become one of the leading long-haul destinations.

Fleming was in Rome when he heard that an offer had been made on the movie rights for *Dr. No*. He took the Laguna Express, which appears in his short story "Risico", to Venice, where he intended to have second honeymoon with Ann. Tactlessly, to help her get to know the city, he gave her a copy of Thomas Mann's *Death in Venice*.

The negotiations over the *Dr. No* movie were put on hold when CBS then proposed a thirteen-part James Bond series. This fell through, leaving the movie option free and clear again.

Now fifty, Fleming was feeling increasingly unwell. He was still smoking sixty a day and his doctors told him to cut down. Alone Goldeneye that winter, he completed a book of five short Bond stories published as *For Your Eyes Only* in 1960. Work ceased when Ann turned up, determined to see off Blanche.

As the critics panned *Goldfinger*, it raced to the top of the best-sellers' list. Then Kemsley sold the loss-making *Sunday Times* to Lord Thomson, but Fleming was retained for his editorial input and the occasional feature. Meanwhile he spent more time working on his private passion, the *Book Collector*.

Chapter Ten – Bond at the Box Office

It seemed clear to everyone concerned that James Bond was destined for the silver screen. But how to get him there? Ivar Bryce had set up a film studio on the Bahamas with one-time producer Kevin McClory to take advantage of tax breaks there and Fleming was called in to write a screenplay from a hastily written plot outline provided by Ernie Cuneo. This would become *Thunderball*.

In the early Bond novels, the enemy had been SMERSH, the real-life name of a Soviet counter-intelligence agency founded in 1943. But Fleming was convinced that the Cold War might end while the film was in production, so SMERSH was replaced with SPECTRE – the Special Executive for Counterintelligence, Terrorism, Revenge and Extortion, manned by ex-members of SMERSH, former Nazis, Chinese Tongs and members of the Mafia.

Fleming completed a sixty-seven page treatment before returning to London. Then he travelled into East Germany with an old intelligence colleague and moved on to Hong Kong and Macao, ostensibly to write an article for the *Sunday Times*. In Tokyo, Richard Hughes introduced him to journalist Torao Saito, known as "Tiger" who took him to a geisha house. This features in *You Only Live Twice*. Hughes becomes Dikko Henderson, Australia's man in Tokyo, and Saito Tiger Tanaka appears as head of the Japanese

Secret Service. The book was also dedicated to "Richard Hughes and Torao Saito, But for whom etc.…".

Returning to Goldeneye, Fleming completed another Bond book – *Thunderball* – which was dedicated to "Ernest Cuneo, Muse". Later that year, Fleming was in Washington where he dined with presidential hopeful John F. Kennedy, who picked his brain on how to handle Fidel Castro, the new dictator of Cuba. Kennedy then included *From Russia With Love* among his top ten books in *Life* magazine. Overnight, Fleming became the top-selling thriller writer in the US.

Quitting his post at the *Sunday Times*, he continued write his "Eight Adventures" series – now called "Thrilling Cities". In Hamburg, he sampled the sex industry. In Berlin, he crossed the Wall. In Switzerland, he dined with Charlie Chaplin, securing the serialization rights to Chaplin's memoirs for the *Sunday Times*. Then in Naples, he had tea with Lucky Luciano.

In Beirut, Fleming talked about Kim Philby, who he had known since his days at Reuters, with the local SIS head. Soon after, Philby defected. Fleming moved on to Kuwait, where he had been commissioned to write the non-fiction book *State of Excitement*. After reading the manuscript, the Kuwait Oil Company rejected it and it was never published.

The next Bond book, *The Spy Who Loved Me*, was written from the point-of-view of the heroine. It was Ann's idea and Fleming said it was the easiest thing he ever wrote. But when it was published he admitted that it was an experiment that had "gone awry" and tried to restrict any reprints or paperback editions. Again he toyed with the idea of killing Bond off.

But trouble was looming. When Kevin McClory saw an advanced copy of the novel *Thunderball*, he claimed it was based on the film scripts he and others had been working on and sued for breach of copyright. Then, at the age of fifty-three, Fleming had a heart attack. Recuperating in hospital he wrote a bedtime story for his son Caspar, which became *Chitty Chitty Bang Bang: The Magical Car*. After Fleming died, Roald Dahl wrote the script for the movie, produced by Cubby Broccoli, co-producer of the Bond films.

Harry Saltzman, a Canadian producer based in London, had acquired a movie option on the Bond books. Teaming up with American émigré, Albert R. "Cubby" Broccoli, they formed Eon Productions to handle the Bond project and signed a deal with United Artists for six Bond movies. The first to go into production was to have been *Thunderball*, but due to legal problems they chose *Dr. No* instead.

After convalescing in Province, Fleming returned to London and suggested his old friend David Niven play James Bond. It was pointed out that Niven was too old and, as an established Hollywood star, too expensive. So Fleming opted for Roger Moore, then playing *The Saint* on TV. When Sean Connery was picked instead, Fleming called him "that fucking truck driver" after his role in the 1957 B-movie *Hell Drivers*. Fleming thought that the working-class Scottish actor did not have the necessary social graces to play is hero, but female friends assured him that Connery had "it".

Fleming recommended that they use Blanche's son Chris Blackwell as location manager for the movie. With Fleming's blessing, he also advised on authentic Jamaican music for the soundtrack and went on to found Island Records, which introduced Bob Marley to the world.

While at the *Sunday Times*, Fleming had commissioned a series of articles on the Seven Deadly Sins. When these were published in book form, Fleming provided an introduction by Ian. He also wrote an introduction to a new edition of one of his favourite novels, *All Night at Mr Stanyhurst's* by Hugh Edwards. Fleming's short story "The Living Daylights" appeared in the first edition of the *Sunday Times* colour supplement. In it, the female Russian assassin was based on his half-sister Amaryllis, his mother's daughter by Augustus John. Bond refuses to shoot her.

In the next novel to come out of Goldeneye, *On Her Majesty's Secret Service*, Bond adopts the identity of Hilary Bray – the name of a friend he had known since school days. The son of a friend at the College of Arms, who bore the glorious title "Rouge Dragon Pursuivant", did the genealogical research for the book and discovered that the Bonds of Peckham had the family motto "The world is not enough", which would become the title of a Bond movie. The Rouge Dragon was not amused to see the name of his heraldic office used in the manuscript, so Fleming changed it to the fanciful Griffon Or Pursuivant and invented another heraldic office known as Sable Basilisk on the grounds that the mythical basilisk looks like a dragon and his friend lived in Basil Street.

The book also contains the story of a man given a peerage for "political and public services – i.e. charities and party funds" who wants to call himself Lord Bentley Royal after a village in Essex. However, it was explained to him that the word "Royal" could only be used by the reigning family. Then the College of Arms mischievously pointed that that the title "Lord Bentley Common" was available. The same story had been told about Lord Kemsley who lived in Farnham. *OHMSS* also drew on Fleming's visit to St Moritz the previous year.

While Fleming dismissed his Bond books as "adolescent" in press, the Soviet newspaper *Izvestia* condemned Bond as a tool of American propaganda and Fleming was asked to comment on real-life intelligence matters such as the return of spy-plane pilot Gary Powers who had been shot down over the Soviet Union. He also had a brush with danger when he went to see the shooting of the iconic scene in *Dr. No* where Ursula Andress emerges from the sea. He was with Ann, Peter Quennell and Stephen Spender when, in the scene, shots were fired. Fleming and his guests were found later cowering spread-eagled in the sand.

While sitting for a portrait by engineer-turned-artist Amherst Villiers, Fleming was introduced to racing driver Graham Hill and used details from their conversations in his descriptions of Bond's cars. By then he worked just two days a week and spent most of his time playing bridge or golf. He presented the "James Bond All Purpose Grand Challenge Vase" to the Old Etonian Golfing Society. It was a chamber pot.

Fleeing the strains of his marriage, Fleming took another trip alone to Jamaica in July 1963, where he began work on the short story "Octopussy" – taking the name from a boat that Blanche had brought to Goldeneye. While he was there, he wrote the introduction to the biography of Sir William Stephenson, *The Quiet Canadian*, then headed back to Japan to research his next Bond book, *You Only Live Twice*.

In Tokyo, he visited Ketels, the bar where Soviet spy Richard Sorge had picked up secrets from Nazi expatriates during World War II. He also immersed himself in Japanese culture, showing particularly interest in the girls from Mikimoto's Island who dived for pearls, traditionally naked. When Bond goes missing in the book, M wrote his obituary for *The Times* where Fleming seized the chance to spoof himself, saying: "The inevitable publicity, particularly in the foreign Press, accorded some of these adventures, made him, much against his will, something of a public figure, with the inevitable result that a series of popular books came to be written around him by a personal friend and former colleague of James Bond. If the quality of these books, or their degree of veracity, had been any higher, the author would certainly have been prosecuted under the Official Secrets Act."

In fact, in 1959, when interest was first being show in making a film of a James Bond novel, Fleming got clearance from the Foreign Office.

On Her Majesty's Secret Service was well received. At the same time Cyril Connolly's homosexual spoof *Bond Strikes Camp* came out in *London Magazine*. In it, Bond dresses in drag and penetrates the "Homintern" to mask a traitor, who turns out to be M. Fleming was delighted by the parody and even made slight amendments to the manuscript before publication.

Fleming returned to Istanbul to see the filming of *From Russia With Love*, but was back in London in time to see the downfall of his friend Defence Minister John Profumo, who had been caught sharing a young mistress with a Russian spy. It could have been a plotline in a Bond novel. He lunched with Allen Dulles who had recently retired as head of the CIA. The author of *The Craft of Intelligence*, Dulles had recommended the Bond books to a gathering of the American Booksellers' Association, so Fleming dubbed him 008.

Oxford University began a James Bond Club, while two editors of the *Harvard Lampoon* wrote a seventy-page spoof called *Alligator*. Then Fleming received the final accolade – an appearance on the BBC's radio programme *Desert Island Discs*, but feared his record selection was "too light-hearted".

For Sotheby's house magazine *The Ivory Hammer* he wrote the short story "The Property of a Lady" which was incorporated into the plot of the film *Octopussy*. Meanwhile forty-four volumes from his book collection went on display at the exhibition "Printing and the Mind of Man". It was by far the largest contribution from a private individual.

While driving to Switzerland to interview Georges Simenon for the *Sunday Times*, Fleming gave a terrified Blanche a high-speed tour of the haunts of his youth in his new Studebaker Avanti. Back in

London, the court case over the rights to *Thunderball* began. After a backroom deal, McClory won the movie rights, while Fleming held on to the rights in the novel, which is now accredited as "based on a screen treatment by Kevin McClory, Jack Whittingham, and Ian Fleming".

Although Fleming was now in constant pain from angina and under strict instructions from a coronary specialist to avoid smoking, alcohol and exertion, he took off for Jamaica again that winter to write *The Man With The Golden Gun*. Having been given up for dead by the Secret Service at the end of *You Only Live Twice*, Bond is resurrected again. The villain's name Scaramanga, like Blofeld, was taken from a contemporary at Eton.

Fleming worked with a steely determination, though he could manage no more than an hour at a time. In *You Only Live Twice*, Mary Goodnight suggests an epitaph for Bond: "I shall not waste my days in trying to prolong them. I shall use my time." It was Fleming's motto.

Although he enjoyed the flowers, the birds and the fish more than ever, Goldeneye was not as peaceful as it had been before. A garage had opened nearby with a sound system which often blared out a reggae version of "Three Blind Mice" that had been released on Chris Blackwell's Island label following its use on the soundtrack of *Dr. No*.

Among the visitors that winter was the real James Bond – the American ornithologist whose name Fleming had appropriated. Fleming found Bond and his wife "a charming couple who are amused by the whole joke". He also agreed to write the guidebook *Ian Fleming's Jamaica* for André Deutsch, but in the end only managed to contribute the introduction.

Epilogue – You Only Live Twice

On 11 August 1964, after lunch at the Royal St George's Golf Club and dinner at a nearby hotel with a friend, Fleming collapsed and was rushed to hospital in Canterbury. At 1.30 am the following morning, he was pronounced dead. He was fifty-six. By then, he had written twelve novels and one book of short stories, selling over forty million copies. Two films – *Dr. No* and *From Russia With Love* – had already been made and two more – *Goldfinger* and *Thunderball* – were in production. Another books of short stories, containing "Octopussy", "The Living Daylights" and "The Property of a Lady" would be published in 1966.

But while Fleming was dead, his alter ego James Bond was still very much alive. Fleming himself left a scrapbook of ideas and the beginnings of his unpublished short stories were sold at Sotheby's for £14,300 in 1992. But most of the rights to Fleming's literal output had been assigned to Glidrose Productions, which became Ian Fleming Publications in 1998.

In 1966, Gildrose commissioned South African novelist Geoffrey Jenkins to write another Bond novel called *Per Fine Ounce*. They had worked together at Kemsley and Jenkins followed a synopsis they had discussed that was found among Fleming's papers. The following year, *003½: The Adventures of James Bond Junior* was published.

Kingsley Amis, who had done editorial work on *The Man With the Golden Gun*, then wrote *Colonel Sun* under the pseudonym Robert Markham. Screenwriter Christopher Woods novelized *The Spy Who Loved Me* and *Moonraker* as the films bore little relationship to the original books. Thriller writer John Gardner took over, contributing sixteen books to the Bond series, including two novelizations. American author Raymond Benson added six novels, three novelizations and two short stories to the canon. Sebastian Faulks, Jeffery Deaver and William Boyd all gave their own take on Bond, while Charlie Higson produced a series on the Young Bond. And there have been numerous cartoon strips and graphic novels featuring 007.

The film franchise has gone from strength to strength. In 2014, fifty years after Bond's creator died, the twenty-fourth in the Eon series went into production and Daniel Craig had already signed up to star in *Bond 25*.

Curiously, Fleming himself had had a fictional reincarnation. In 1956, Noël Coward wrote the play *Volcano* about the affair between Ian Fleming and Blanche Blackwell. In 2012 – fifty-six years later – it received its debut on the West End stage. Blanche, by then a hundred, saw the production but declined to comment.

Printed in Great Britain
by Amazon.co.uk, Ltd.,
Marston Gate.